GOLDEN
CLAN

GOLDEN CLAN

The Murrays, the McDonnells,
and the Irish American
Aristocracy

JOHN CORRY

LYONS
PRESS

Essex, Connecticut

An imprint of The Globe Pequot Publishing Group, Inc.
64 South Main Street
Essex, CT 06426
www.globepequot.com

Distributed by NATIONAL BOOK NETWORK

British Library Cataloguing in Publication Information available

Library of Congress Cataloging-in-Publication Data

ISBN 978-1-4930-8691-7 (paper : alk. paper)
ISBN 978-1-4930-8692-4 (electronic)

♾™ The paper used in this publication meets the minimum requirements
of American National Standard for Information Sciences—Permanence of
Paper for Printed Library Materials, ANSI/NISO Z39.48-1992.

For Jeanne

Contents

	Foreword	ix
	Preface	xvii
I	The Patriarch	1
II	Propriety and Piety	22
III	Tom's Children	37
IV	Grandees and Climbers	55
V	Southampton: Days of Grace	69
VI	Cardinals, Priests, and Acolytes	87
VII	Aristocrats at Last	101
VIII	Barons and Buccaneers	124
IX	Rites of Passage	141
X	An Irish Requiem	158
XI	Profit and Loss	175
	Illustrations	189
	Index	191

Foreword

WHEN I was born in 1953, the population of the United States was 160,184,192 and approximately 25 percent Catholic. Waves of immigrants arrived from Europe between 1800 and 1914, including Italian Catholics and German Catholics. They were never referred to as "Italian Catholics" or "German Catholics." They were simply Italians or Germans. But the Irish earned the double moniker of "Irish Catholic," when being referred to as simply "Irish" would have sufficed.

John Corry's *Golden Clan* begins at a time in America when the Irish were still accepted co-partners in settling the New World. They were enterprising adventurers with enough brains and resources to make their mark. Though some of these Irish were Catholic, and a few Protestants, the prejudices against Catholics had yet to crystalize in the New World and the possibilities for Irish Catholics were still boundless.

Corry then summarizes the injustices visited upon Irish Catholics by the British through a series of laws that were enacted from 1607 to 1771 to punish Irish Catholics for being Catholic. Catholics were prohibited from being educated, leasing land for more than thirty-one years, indulging in commerce, speaking Gaelic, owning a gun, marrying a Protestant, or voting. Collectively, these laws were referred to as the "Penal Laws."

The English colonies in America each practiced their own version of religious preference, but the majority recognized the supremacy of Anglicanism over alternative faith and the power to discriminate against non-Anglicans was invested in each colony's governing body. This was particularly so in Virginia, North and South Carolina, and Georgia. Massachusetts was governed under a Puritan theocracy which promoted Congregationalism, but did not tolerate papists. Connecticut adopted Congregationalism as its official religion and even tolerated Quakers, but no relief was granted to papists until 1741. Rhode Island, Pennsylvania, and Delaware chose a clear separation of Church and State, and both Maryland and New Jersey eventually did the same.

However, prior to 1763, Marylanders still paid a twenty-shilling tax for each imported Irish domestic servant, Catholic mothers could lose their children if their Protestant husband died, Maryland's Capitol was transferred from St. Mary's, then a Catholic enclave, to primarily Protestant Annapolis, priests could not say Mass, and many Catholics turned to Europe for the Catholic education that was denied them in the colonies. That period supplied the kernel of prejudice that grew into a general disapproval of Irish Catholic immigrants who soon arrived in the wake of the potato blights, the worst of which were in 1845 and 1879.

These were the "Shanty Irish" who inspired nicknames like Bog Jumper, Coal Cracker, Pot Licker, Mackerel Snapper, Potato Eater and Mucker, or, as I was once called by a neighbor, Filthy Mick. I was filthy because we were playing football, but I had to ask my mother about the "Mick" part, and she took a deep, calming breath before dispatching my older brother, George, to correct the offender, the son of a prominent Youngstown, Ohio, steel executive. That was in 1961, approximately 100 years after my great-grandfather made the trip from Cork, Ireland, to New Hampshire. While I was never called a Filthy Mick again, at least to my face, my parents took pains to enlighten us as to the struggles, the failures, and the disappointments that Irish Catholics faced in their climb out of poverty.

Our Youngstown, Ohio, home was a shrine to Catholicism, starting at the front door where you were met by flanking portraits of recent popes—Pope Pius XII and Pope John XXIII. There were crosses over our beds which were tucked behind the white-green fronds from the last Palm Sunday. Each May, my mother converted a dresser into a May Altar by draping a blue sheet over a stack of books, and topping the ziggurat with candles, daffodils, and a statue of the Virgin Mary.

My mom and dad would gather all nine children kneeling before the May Altar with our rosaries, where we would project our pious best while secretly calculating exactly how many Hail Marys and Our Fathers remained before we were released. We never ate meat on Fridays and we always went to Mass on Sunday with empty stomachs. My dad went to Mass every morning, except Saturday, and both my mother and dad knelt in prayer by their bed every night. As altar boys, we had to master the Mass in Latin so the priest would not clip us with his wingtips for botching a Latin phrase.

The struggles of the Shanty Irish in America made great copy, as evidenced in works by Jim Tully, *Shanty Irish*; Jeanne Charters, *Shanty Gold (Daughter of Ireland)*; and books by Maeve Binchy, Sean O'Casey, John Synge, and others. However, a few authors focused their attention several rungs higher up the social ladder on those who not only climbed out of poverty, but who outdid the cultish rituals of the socially upright Protestants. One can find this in John O'Hara's short stories; John Corry's *Golden Clan* is a tour de force of this genre.

Corry was born in 1933 in Brooklyn to Irish Episcopalian parents whose ancestors changed Curry to Corry because they thought it sounded more Protestant. He graduated from Hope College in 1954 and spent two years in the Army before commencing a thirty-one-year career with the *New York Times*.

At the *New York Times*, he once devoted an entire year reporting on the residents of a single block on West 85th Street in Manhattan. The results appeared under a column entitled

"City Block." This approach was akin to focusing the Hubble Space Telescope on a speck of the outer universe only to discover millions of sub-subjects within. In *Golden Clan*, he focuses that same investigative intensity on the Murray clan to capture the cohesive forces used by Irish Catholics at the time to attain a measure of respect from a country that was loath to offer them any.

Somewhere in his career, he found a sixth gear for clarity, humor, and style which kept his writing from devolving into a long-winded society column that fawned over the oddities of the rich and famous. And while *Golden Clan* had plenty of material of that ilk, he lingered longer on the character within his characters, particularly the discipline they derived from their Catholic beliefs.

As an Irish Catholic, I rarely gave much thought to my upbringing before reading *Golden Clan*. At first, I was amused by the obsession of the Real Lace Irish, or, as Corry deems them, "the Irish Aristocracy" on being perfect, perfectly devout, clean, educated, punctual, honest, polite, and loyal. But then I realized he was describing the Irish Catholic families of my youth. In fact, I never needed to say I was Irish Catholic, only that I was the seventh of nine children, or that my dad was the first of ten children, and that declaration normally garnered a polite and knowing nod.

Corry's champion in *Golden Clan* is Thomas Murray, who was born in Albany in 1860 and who worked his way up from lighting gas lamps to building the largest power generation plants in the country, culminating with the creation of Consolidated Edison. His eight children were raised in the Catholic tradition, as were his thirty-eight grandchildren, and the family slowly built an all–Irish Catholic protectorate that straddled Albany, Manhattan, and Southampton, New York.

John Corry takes readers through the carefully curated upbringing of the Murrays and their children with emphasis on the power the matriarchs had in raising their children. He also observes how the petty slights of non-Catholics unleashed an urge to produce children who were an improved version of the best the Protestants had to offer. Any deviation from strict maternal norms was considered a threat to respectability, and respectability was the currency they amassed in their quest for greater social status in America.

Corry's description of the Murray family's adherence to the strict proprieties of an Irish Catholic upbringing seems over-wrought in retrospect, but they were the norm of the time for Irish Catholics nationwide. They were certainly embraced by the Catholic families I knew growing up, both rich and poor, and the Church was absolutely at the center of that universe.

A good deal has changed since Thomas Murray said rosaries with his daughters' dates before they were allowed out of the house. Families of seven to twelve children are now rare, and many of the ascetic requirements of being Catholic have given way to modernism.

Prior to 1964, Catholic masses were as uniform as McDonald's hamburgers, whether you were attending mass at Saints Faith, Hope & Charity in Winnetka, or St. Patrick's in Manhattan. Priests and nuns were holy people who were deemed to be closer to God than the congregants and were granted unquestioned respect and authority. Being Catholic still required strict adherence to a litany of obligations, many of which were coupled with a threat of damnation, if ignored. There was order, discipline, and direction, and there was comfort in belonging to a community doggedly hewing to the ways of being a good Catholic, some of which were also amusing.

My mom had a great chuckle that would devolve into an eye water snort if encouraged. If a sermon was dragging but provided an opportunity for a humorous aside to mom, we would all watch her, head bent, hand over mouth as her shoulders shuddered in her attempt to suppress an outburst. My dad would quietly pass his silver rosaries to the culprit. I also learned to scrape my feet along the carpet at St. Edwards when holding the brass patent for the priest during communion. As soon as a classmate stuck their tongue out for communion, I would unleash the built-up static electricity by tapping the edge of the patent to their throat.

My mother was taught philosophy at Rosemont College by Bishop Fulton Sheen, who had a nationally televised broadcast called *Life Is Worth Living*. Bishop Sheen was credited with converting Clare Booth Luce to Catholicism after her daughter, Ann Clare Brokow, died at the age of twenty-two in a car accident. In 1961, Mrs. Luce was invited to address the Junior League in Youngstown and stayed at our home the evening before. My older brother, Jake, then six, bounded home from school to meet the famous woman but was told that she was indisposed. Undeterred, Jake found her in the bath where she was heard saying, "Go away little man, Auntie Clare is taking her bath, now go away!"

And there were downsides to being Catholic. For example, in certain Catholic schools, transcripts from students with Ivy potential miraculously only found their way to Catholic colleges—Holy Cross, Manhattanville, Boston College, Fairfield, Georgetown, Fordham, St. Mary's, or Rosemont. Certain clubs and neighborhoods quietly nurtured anti-Catholic policies and some communities aggressively limited the leadership positions available to Catholics, particularly in the Northeast.

In 1962, Pope John XXIII realized that the conservative ways of the Church were out of step with the modern world, so he initiated a series of forums to evaluate ways to make the Church more relevant. Those forums took place from 1962 to 1965 and were referred to as Vatican II.

Some of the changes from Vatican II were welcomed. Priests now face the congregation, Latin was set aside for the local vernacular, and the mournful dirges of the lady on the organ in the back of the church were replaced by smiling guitarists doggedly coaxing toneless congregants into song. Lay people are involved in the Mass, and Masses differ church by church. Some held to a solemn tone, others took on hootenanny theatrics. One's faith journey is now more a matter of personal autonomy than a blind obedience to the strictures of the Church.

And there were some not-so-wonderful results as far as some of the affected were concerned. Nuns were demoted to the status of parishioners and were no longer required to wear habits—ninety thousand left the Church. While abortion was never condoned, in 1968, Pope Paul VI's *Humanae Vitae* declared birth control a moral offense. His timing was a bit off because women were finally slipping their domestic shackles and were less enthralled by the notion of blind obedience to the Church, particularly on birth control. Then there is the slow dissipation by intermarriage with alternative faiths, or no faith at all, coupled with a general secularization away from religion. For me and many disappointed Catholics, the Church's lackadaisical response to pedophiles within its ranks justified a general exodus.

Still, the Catholic Church remains vibrant and necessary in a world that is increasingly infatuated with all things amoral. While the hairshirts and ascetic ways of the past have been relaxed, the results of the Catholic tradition remain all around us in its churches and schools and charitable programs and in the stories of its champions, such as the Murray family.

This book is filled with stories of fortunes made and lost, scoundrels and saints, and while it is told through the lives of several Irish Catholic families, it is really about America coming of age. I hope you enjoy the stories behind the Golden Clan as much as you will John Corry's wonderful style of writing.

—James F. Coakley
Alexandria, Virginia
May 2024

Preface

JOHN CORRY always said he wanted his daughters to be as comfortable with his secretary as the Queen of England. He took great pride in exposing us to both worlds—introducing us to the receptionists at the *New York Times* where he worked, while also putting us in front of the various people he interviewed—including an actual prince and princess, with whom he insisted we share our cookies.

He also raised us to know we were—with no question—"Irish Protestant." This was pronounced as one word, "Irish-Protestant," as if one was inseparable from the other. It wasn't until I was a teenager that I learned that indeed, it was possible for someone to be Protestant and French—or Irish and Catholic. "IrishProtestant" was who we were, and who we should always be proud to be. So what in the world was he doing writing a book about the well, the unspeakable "other"? I suspect it had something to do with the very fact they *were* the other.

John grew up in Bay Ridge, Brooklyn, when it was a gritty, toughened affair, a working class neighborhood. People lived and died there without leaving. At least, that was the neighborhood he would describe to my sister and me as we rode the subway from Manhattan to visit his mother.

As the subway stops rolled by, he would tell us story after story. (He was a brilliant storyteller—in print, yes, but even more so in person. And while some stories may have been slightly embellished, they all were dynamic, entertaining, and always had a curious blend of a boisterous self-regard and raw self-deprecation.) Colette and I would sit rapt as he wove tales about his life there—playing stick ball in the street, buying bubble gum to trade, and his (exaggerated, I suspect) success as a champion yo-yo player.

His father, a bank teller, and his mother, a secretary, took their Protestant faith very seriously—even managing to save enough money to install a stained-glass window at their church—which is there to this day. As a child, I believe John (or "Johnny" as he was called then) was marched there every Sunday to pray.

Sometimes we would go to that same church when we visited our grandmother. During services, I'm not sure he even sang the hymns, but it was clear: "THIS is your heritage." And while "Johnny" apparently had pride in his family's place there, I never got the impression it was the religion that mattered as much to my father as the identity.

It was on the rides back we heard some of the darker side of Bay Ridge. Poverty. Street gangs: Italian. Norwegian.

Irish.

The Irish had two factions, and mixing was not tolerated. The Protestants kept separate from the Catholics, and the Catholics kept separate from the Protestants. In fact, John told us once about a brutal fight between the two groups, and even his normally animated storytelling was subdued. But then we would be back in Manhattan, and life—and John—would be chatty and relaxed again. Somehow, even as a young girl, I knew those subway rides were taking us between different worlds. He loved New York, and everything that made it itself. But he loved Manhattan best.

Brooklyn was, for him, a place of his childhood and, I suspect, limitations. It was a long ride for a kid from Bay Ridge to the newsroom he had longed for. Manhattan was where he could fulfill his dream of being a writer for the *New York Times* and live a life of words and intellect, glamour and freedom.

People fascinated him. He was, in every sense of the word, a reporter. He loved to watch everyone around him and speculate. When he took us to restaurants, he would encourage us to listen in on nearby tables without looking, and see if we could guess the age, the country, or anything at all about the people speaking. For several years he wrote "About New York," a weekly column about the people and places that made New York City what it was. He went with cops on raids, and described once using his ballpoint pen, thrust menacingly in his pocket, at a suspect while the raiding team hid in the shadow doubled over in laughter. He wrote about the animal keepers at the zoo, and the violinist at the Plaza Hotel. He wrote about the mayor, and the street cleaners. He wrote about lonely women, and divorced men putting their children on the crosstown bus back to their mothers, and away from them. He wrote because it was what he was born to do.

So why then of all the people and places in New York, did he decide on the "Golden Clan"? I will never be able to ask him, but I think since his identity as "Irish Protestant" was so very much a part of his upbringing, celebrating the "Irish Catholic" may have been a kind of liberation. Perhaps there was even a little bit of rebellion in the research—as if to thumb his nose and tell his parents, "See? I can be different." To research and write about the "Others"—and to do so with affection and care—was definitively to say: "I am no longer only that boy in Bay Ridge. I can talk and walk with the elite of the city, and be exactly who I choose to be."

My father did not want to be stuck as one thing or another. Like the Irish Catholic you will meet in this book, John Corry was raised to be "one identity"—and also understood we can be so much more. There may be magic, and meaning, and wonderful tales to tell—but at the end of the day, we are all a gloriously and perfectly messy community of humans.

And like his desire to introduce his daughters to receptionists and royalty, I believe my father would want you to be interested in *everyone* in this book—from the troubled Daniel Murray, to the supremely organized and well-coiffed Mrs. Anna Murray.

If he were with us, I suspect he would ask *you* what you think of everyone, and if you can say more about their stories (peeking at their pictures definitely allowed). I know he loved learning about "Catholic royalty" and had great fun researching and writing this book. I feel sure he would be delighted to know it is in your hands.

—Janet Farnsworth

I

The Patriarch

THE FIRST of the Irish arrived only a few at a time, and the wonder is that they chose to go there at all. Albany, New York, was Dutch, and the Dutch, not being greatly known for their hospitality, and speaking a language full of sounds made from behind the epiglottis, hardly seemed like suitable neighbors for the Gaels. Still, the Irish came anyway, and usually they only endured, but sometimes they even prevailed. John Anderson of Dublin arrived in Albany in 1645, and through some charm all his own was made a burgher. He farmed, sold liquor, and became known as "Johnny the Irishman." A few years after him, John Connel opened an inn, and then Thomas Parvel became a baker, and then William Hogan opened an inn, and then John Finn did, too. Finn, however, was litigious, forever turning up in court with this grievance or that, and once suing a farmer because he thought the farmer had slandered his wife. A nuisance, the Dutch call Finn, a *Gottdamn* nuisance.

Now these, of course, were not your ordinary Irishmen, your ordinary Irishman then being a person of no substance whatsoever, more likely to be driving a cart or cleaning out a stable than to be doing anything of importance, and almost certain to leave nothing behind him when he died. Indeed the poor Irishman in Albany left only his name and sometimes not even that. It was curious: the Irish men married Dutch girls and begat daughters and more daughters, and not many sons. The Irish names disappeared, and it seemed that the Irish were losing again, which was really all they had been doing since they had beaten the Danes at Clontarf in 1014. Nonetheless, the Irish kept coming over to Albany, a man alone, and now and then a husband and wife, and by the time of the Revolution there were Irish all about the place.

In time, Irish was to mean Catholic, and it would be understood that if you were Irish the Catholic part simply followed. When the country was young, however, being Irish meant that you could be Scotch Irish, too. The grandparents and great-grandparents of these Scotch Irish were Scots, who had been settled in Ireland by the English to shed the light of Protestantism over that wild land, and the grandchildren and great-grandchildren who came here were Presbyterian and Church of England. Still, they were considered Irish, and in those days there was no great stigma attached to being Irish, even if there was plenty to being Catholic. In 1802, the Scotch Irish and the Catholic Irish in Albany even got together long enough to form the United Irish and Scotch Benevolent Society, although forming it was all they ever did. A year later, the Scotch Irish marched out, leaving the Catholic Irish to themselves, and organized the St. Andrew's Society. A few years after that, however, the Catholic Irish in Albany, deciding to "afford relief to indigent and distressed emigrants from the kingdom of Ireland," formed a St. Patrick's Society.

In a few years they were celebrating St. Patrick's Day, and since these were mostly respectable Irish, even if they were Catholic, and not the wild kind who came swarming up the Erie Canal a little later, the Mayor of Albany and Governor of New York attended their affairs. In fact, "the celebrated Irish patriot, orator and lawyer, Thomas Addis Emmet, whose attendance was a distinguished mark of consideration and evidence of the importance of the Irish in Albany and their high standing and character as citizens," was at one, too. At that particular party everyone drank eighteen toasts, first to noble sentiments, and then to people and things, and finally to the fairies and leprechauns themselves. It was forty years before there was a big celebration of St. Patrick's Day in Albany again.

By 1825, when the Erie Canal reached Albany, there were perhaps 100,000 Catholics in New York State, with about 50,000 of them, nearly all Irish, living along the path of the canal. The work on the canal had begun in 1817, and within a year 3000 Irishmen were at it, doing the foul jobs that no one else wanted to do. At first, they were paid as much as $1.50 a day, but as more Irishmen kept showing up the wages dropped, sometimes to as little as fifty cents a day, and sometimes less. These were lean times, hard times, and the Irish lived in shanties and died in mud slides.´ There were brawls, there were accidents, and fetid whiskey huts were thrown up overnight. Contractors cheated the Irish workers. Rival gangs terrorized them, and missionary priests ministered to them. By 1840, New York had 944 miles of canals, and the Irish had built all of them.

These canal Irish, rude, uncouth, smelling bad, and only lately off the boat, were a different kind of Irish. They bothered the Americans, and they bothered the Irish who had gotten here before them. In 1832, the Albany Hibernian Provident was organized, with its purpose "twofold: to create a fund by a general subscription among the Members, which shall contribute to their mutual advantage if by reason of sickness they should become destitute of the conveniences of life; and also to organize in one body a numerous class of Irishmen residing in this City, and to congregate their moral energies, so as to bring fairly before the American people the Republican features of their national character." In other words, the Irish were not only ragged and broke; they were suspect, too.

This was because there was a question in Albany, as there was in the rest of the country, whether these ditchdiggers, who, in truth, were the most republican of men, were fit for the Great Republic at all. So, Albany watched and waited, and while it did the Irish kept coming. Catholicism, being rather invisible, had not been much of an issue in the earliest days. The Catholics in Albany, Irish and otherwise, had met in someone's home, and it was not until 1797 that the cornerstone of St. Mary's Church was laid. Seven Irishmen were on the board of trustees, and it was only the second Catholic parish in the state. With the coming of the canal Irish, work was begun on a new St. Mary's in 1839. If it was not chic, it was at least respectable, and Talleyrand and Lafayette visited it. Soon, there were St. John's, St. Joseph's, the Church of the Holy Cross (which was for the Germans, who did not get on well with the Irish, with the Gaels finding the Teutons unbearable, too), and eventually the Cathedral of the Immaculate Conception. From the Cathedral, Bishop John McCloskey, a gentle man who was the son of an Irish shopkeeper in Brooklyn, watched over the flock. One day he was to be made the first American Cardinal, greatly annoying the other Bishops, and also unloosing those political and social intrigues in which generations of Catholic matrons would someday take pleasure. "I hope we shall have no Cardinal's hat in this country," McCloskey himself once wrote to Archbishop Martin Spalding of Baltimore. "We are better without one."

By the middle of the century, Albany was a quiet town of 25,000 people, full of old Dutch pride, as it was forever reminding itself, and the sensibilities of the newer people. A man had built the great Delevan House in 1844, just across from the train station on the corner of Steuben and Broadway, and the man, who until then had been a prominent temperance worker, immediately began to sell whiskey. By the middle of the century, an old elm tree at the corner of State and Pearl streets was also famous. Once, the burghers had tied slaves to a ring driven into its trunk; now it was a rendezvous, a place for lovers and children. The largest brewery in the country was in Albany; so was the state capitol. Jenny Lind had been in town twice, and she had sung in the Third Presbyterian Church. Albany had a hospital by 1849, and this was also the year that a state teachers college was built at Lodge and Harvard streets. The first public school had gone up in 1832, not far from the elm tree, although the first schools that charged no tuition at all did not appear until thirty years later. Albany by then was a middling city, neither a good place nor a bad place for an Irish Catholic, and it was there on October 21, 1860, that Thomas Edward Murray was born.

Now the blotting out of familial memories is a common thing among the Irish, much remarked on by those who know them. Some say that the Irish past has been so full of misery that the Irish simply stopped remembering, the habit and burden of memory being too painful for them to bear. Others say that the Irish are a careless people, and little given to reflection. Others, however, say that the Irish, relentless in their search for respectability, and greatly eager to rise above the past, do not look back because they cannot afford to; the past, somehow, may be gaining on them. Whatever the reason, it is a fact that as a man Thomas E. Murray spoke hardly at all of what it was like when he was a boy. His heirs and their heirs would walk with and even marry captains and kings, and he, being the patriarch, would have made it possible. But, few of the heirs would reckon it this way, and they would never know much about him. This disrespect for the past is very Irish.

Murray's father, John, was a carpenter. He was from

people out of County Wexford, and he died when Tom Murray was nine years old. He had another son, whose name also was John, and if Thomas Murray had little to say about his father in years to come, he had nothing at all to say about his brother. In fact, he disapproved of him. John drank. He was what was called a ne'er-do-well. When the father died, he did a bunk, and so young Tom quit school to go to work to support his mother. He had not been attending a public school; he had been taking lessons from a man called Paddy Keenan, and the Murrays, driven by God knows what respectable impulse, had been paying Keenan a tuition of five candles and twenty-five cents a week. So, on the death of his father, Tom found a job with the Albany Gas Company, turning on their streetlights in the evening and extinguishing them in the morning. Electricity then was still a toy, and the incandescent bulb had not even begun to tax Thomas Edison's imagination. In Britain, Michael Faraday already had announced that he had developed a dynamo, although oddly enough Joseph Henry, a mathematics teacher at the Albany Boys' Academy, who later became a professor of physics at Princeton, had done it first. Nonetheless, he had not announced it, and Murray, who one day would build some of the biggest power plants in the world, never even heard of him.

Instead, Murray was to insist that the great influence in his life was his mother, Anastasia. "My dominating ambition was to earn money to help support my mother," he insisted in his later years, and he insisted it with passion. Anastasia, he would say, drove him to newer and greater triumphs. She had succored him and nurtured him, and in the evenings and on Sunday afternoons she had sung old Irish melodies to him. "Those songs you sing," Murray told the great tenor John McCormack, "people think they're new, but my mother sang them to me years ago." Murray was an Irish boy, and he carried the memory, the imprint, really, of his mother forever.

(After Murray's death, a letter writer to the *New York Times* said that a flag flying at half-staff in his honor was actually "a banner proclaiming the love of a boy for his mother.") In time, the priests around Murray would speak of his wife the same way other priests once spoke of his mother. They were both upright and pious women, given to training their children, and trudging to work as a boy Murray would recite the rosary. "I believe in one God, the Father Almighty," he would begin, and go on through all fifteen decades.

There were other influences, too. The Van Rensselaers were the great family in Albany when Murray was a boy, and anyone who had not dined in their manor house near Washington Park was not of much importance. Still, the Talcotts weren't bad either, and one of them became a patron of young Tom Murray's. This was General Sebastian Vissher Talcott, a man much afflicted by the burden of genealogy, which Murray, being Irish, was not. General Talcott, as he was always known, was a graduate of Yale who became a civil engineer and then a surveyor for the Erie Railroad. During the Civil War he was named the Quartermaster General of New York, which obviously suited him since nearly everyone else in the family had a military rank, too. His father, who had also been a general, once commanded the Albany Arsenal, but he was court-martialed for disobeying orders and for what the army called "conduct unbecoming an officer and gentleman." The son later showed a fine family loyalty when he wrote, "The Talcott Pedigree and Genealogical Notes of New York and New England Families" and other works of family history. He never once mentioned the court-martial.

One day, Tom Murray was shoveling snow in front of General Talcott's home, and on a whim the General invited him inside. It was the first time the boy had met an engineer, and he was impressed. The General was also impressed, and he invited young Tom back for dinner. "Tom," he said that night, "I think you'll be President of the United States one day." The other thing about the dinner was that the General served roast beef, which Murray was henceforth to consider fit only for ceremonial occasions, and horse radish, which he had never seen before. Whipped cream, he had thought, why is he giving me whipped cream?

And so young Tom moved upward. When he was twelve or so he built a boiler, getting steam from coal, and hired himself out to unclog the frozen downspouts of Albany's gracious Victorian homes. A year or two later he was out walking and passed a bakery. Inside there was a steam engine that enchanted him. He walked in, asked for a job running it, and was told that he was too young, and what did he know about steam engines, anyway? Annoyed, he returned to the machine shop where he now worked and set about building his own steam engine. He did it on his lunch hours and holidays, early in the morning and late at night, first persuading kind friends to turn lathes for him by hand and then making all the parts for the engine himself. In time he returned to the bakery and asked once more for the job, but there is no justice in these things sometimes and he was turned down once again. As a consolation, he sneaked his steam engine into the Albany science fair, where he won the prize in a competition that was supposed to be open only to college students.

He moved onward. At sixteen, believing that his youth was against him, he grew a mustache to look older. At eighteen, he became an engineer with the Albany waterworks. At twenty-one, he became the chief engineer, running the old pumping station at the foot of Clinton Street, and attracting as he did so the attention of Anthony Nicholas Brady.

If Murray was a genius with machines, Brady was a genius with money, early on in life learning how to get large amounts of it and then using it to get even larger amounts. Brady had been born in 1843 in Lille, France, the son of Nicholas and

Ellen Malone Brady, and had come to the United States as a child. He had been indifferent to the benefits of education, which was just as well because his parents couldn't afford one for him, and so he had gone to work. The legend is that as a boy Brady was working as a bartender in the Delevan House in Albany, and that one day a stranger walked in, mumbling and complaining, and saying that he had imported a great deal of tea, but that having fallen on hard times he was unable to pay the duty on it. Consequently, he said, it was locked up in the customhouse.

It was not for nothing that Brady in years to come would be known as the quintessential self-made man, and so he proposed a deal. He would put up the money to get the tea out of the customhouse, and in turn the stranger would take him in as a partner. It was agreed, and in a short time Brady was the master of a number of tea stores, first in Albany, then in Troy, then in other places in the state, and finally in New York City itself. Brady, in fact, was running some of the first chain stores, although this was of no great importance to him because there was far more money to be made elsewhere.

Quite naturally, these being boom times, he turned to construction, and from there he went on to public works, where many Irish fortunes were begun, and where he learned a thing or two about dealing with politicians. Brady was offered contracts to build sewers, sidewalks, and roads. He got control of some granite quarries, and soon he was supplying his own raw materials. He was making a lot of money, and he would make even more when he went into transportation. Eventually, this stocky, florid man would become what was known as a traction magnate, first in Providence, Rhode Island, and Upstate New York, and then in New York City, where he would have as much to say as anyone about where the subways would be built. Brady was an operator, buying and selling politicians at a time when many successful men were doing it, only he was doing it bigger. When he died in 1913, the patriarch of a family that is with us still, he left behind him something like $200 million, which a surrogate judge in Albany somehow appraised for tax purposes at only $80 million. When he first noticed Thomas E. Murray, however, Brady was mostly interested in the possibilities of the new electric light.

Albany had gotten its first streetlights in 1771, when the men who ran the town appropriated the money for twenty oil lamps. In 1841, the Albany Gaslight Company was formed, and within a year it had put burners on ninety old oil lamps. Then, in 1872, something called the Peoples Gaslight Company was formed and consolidated with the old Albany Gaslight Company. This was Tom Murray's first employer. Nonetheless, gas was on the way out, which enterprising men like Brady suspected, and the country was about to undergo a revolution. In 1878, in Menlo Park, New Jersey, the Edison Electric Light Company was born. By 1879, Thomas Edison had perfected the incandescent lamp, and in the same year he and his colleagues designed a complete system for the distribution of electricity. It was really an astonishing feat.

They had to plan a system of conductors that could be placed either above the ground or below it. They had to invent meters. They had to build dynamos larger and more efficient than any yet made, and they had to invent all the appurtenances, even the simplest ones, that went into lighting a home. They did all these things, and in 1880, with its first generating plant in a downtown slum, and with only fifty-nine customers, the Edison Electric Illuminating Company of New York was organized. By then, there had been something like fifty attempts to set up commercial arc lighting systems and they had all failed. Indeed, when Edison talked of "indefinitely subdividing" the electric current, eminent scientists said it was impossible. They were wrong and he went ahead, and there was the revolution.

In Albany, Brady offered Murray a job with the Municipal Gaslight Company, which, despite its name, was involving itself with electricity. Murray was put in charge of the power plant, and eventually Brady began to use him as a consultant on his other projects. There were street railways in Troy, Albany, and Providence, and there were the beginnings of electric companies throughout New York State. This was when technology was new, and when not only entrepreneurs like Brady could rise up from small beginnings; engineers and inventors could, too. The time was right, and Murray was coming up in life.

Soon, Murray was running the Municipal Gas Company. Then, in 1881, the Albany Electric Illuminating Company was organized. Brady had a hand in that, too, and it got a contract to light the streets of Albany. Within a year it had strewn the new electric lights about the capitol building, and a year after that it had all 473 streetlamps in Albany on for ten and a half hours a night. Albany had gotten the telephone only a short time before, and although it did not have sewers in every part of town, the neighborhood where the Irish lived being the last to get them, it was certainly getting the new technology. In 1887, Brady made Murray the general manager of the Albany Electric Illuminating Company, and Murray, ready at last to build his own patrimony, chose to take a wife.

From the beginning, it had been the most Irish Catholic of romances. Thomas E. Murray and Catherine Bradley had met in church. They had sung in the choir of the Cathedral of the Immaculate Conception, and there in the choir loft, surrounded by an acre of imitation stone, overlooking the burnished brass of the high altar, they had fallen in love. Catherine was the daughter of Daniel Bradley, the State Senator from Brooklyn, which, in those long-gone days, meant she was the daughter of someone of stature. Bradley was called "Honest Dan." He carried a walking stick, and when he campaigned in the Irish Catholic wards of Brooklyn he turned his collar around, thereby reminding his people that he was devoted to the church, and perhaps — who knows? — even being mistaken for a priest himself. When Thomas Murray married his daughter, the ceremony was solemnized by the first nuptial mass ever held in Brooklyn. This may not sound like much now, but it was a sure sign then that this was no ordinary union. There was even talk that Murray, who had been just a poor boy, was committing the worst of all the secular sins among the Irish Catholics; he was getting above himself, as they used to say, and who did he think he was, anyway? "Ah," a neighbor told a neighbor, who passed it on to the Bradleys, "she didn't do so well for herself, did she?" The neighbor had just seen Thomas Murray, newly married to his Catherine, walking down a street in Albany. Tom was a swarthy man, one of what was sometimes called the "black Irish," and his mother was a poor widow woman. Who did he think he was, indeed?

Thomas and Catherine built a home in Albany on Madison Avenue, and it was, of course, close to their church. Murray hung it with electric lights, and it had a stained-glass window that was a copy of the west window in the Cathedral of the Immaculate Conception. The Protestant neighbors thought there was an altar behind it. Soon, the children began arriving. First, there was Daniel, then Joseph, Thomas Jr., Catherine, Anna, Julia, and John, and the wonder was that there was time for any children at all. Murray, having worked out an arrangement with an engineer on the New York Central, was commuting every day to New York. Rounding a curve at 140th Street, the train would slow down, and Murray would jump off, ready to go about the work of putting together the electrical empire of Anthony Nicholas Brady.

Brady had gone to New York with a plan, and it had been simplicity itself. There were five or six gas companies competing with one another, and perhaps twice that many electric companies. Everyone knew that in time the gas companies would expire, and the question was what to do about it. Brady wanted Russell Sage, William Rockefeller, and J. Pierpont Morgan to arrange a merger of the gas companies, and then to use the new monopoly to take over the electric companies. This was done, there being some hanky-panky in the state legislature to go with it, and the new monopoly, the Consolidated Gas Company, which later became Consolidated Edison, soon controlled both gas and electricity. Murray was supposed to put together Brady's electrical interests in the operation.

Soon, commuting from Albany palled for Murray, and shortly before 1900 he moved his family to Brooklyn. There had been a community of Irish Catholics there for years, and in the early days they had worked in the Brooklyn Navy Yard as laborers and lived huddled around the Navy Yard and along the waterfront. In 1823, they built a small church for themselves, but before that they had taken a ferry to Manhattan and attended St. Peter's. One of their children was to become Cardinal McCloskey, another the Bishop of Kentucky, and a third the first head of the American College in Rome. Consequently, the Irish Catholics were long established in Brooklyn, although they were not much in evidence in Brooklyn Heights. This was where anyone with social pretensions lived in Brooklyn, and the people with the old Dutch names there even looked down on Manhattan society as arriviste. Murray, who would not have cared for that life anyway, moved his family to St. Mark's Avenue in Crown Heights.

It was solid and comfortable there, a place in the final flowering of those innocent days before World War I, when respectability was a goodness and a Protestant God was running things. St. Mark's Avenue was a little different, though, because it allowed Jews and Catholics in.

Thomas Murray and his family moved first into a brownstone, and then, their prosperity increasing, into a larger house of brick. It was full of dark wood, Tiffany lamps, and hired help. At first, there were only the cook, waitress, and chambermaid; soon there was a butler, a housemaid, and a chauffeur, too. All of them were Irish. There was roast beef every Sunday, and at Christmas a tree that poked itself up the stairwell to the second floor. The last child, Marie, was born, and now there were eight little Murrays. In Albany they had played around a coal pile; in Brooklyn it was different. There the boys wore caps and jackets and the girls had ribbons in their hair, yards of ruffles, and for such small children such great big hats.

Of course, they would all have Catholic educations, and when the children were very young they went to Our Lady of Victory. Then the boys went to St. Francis Xavier in Manhattan and the girls to the Visitation Convent. They all took elocution lessons. They all had to play the piano. When the father or mother had a birthday, they would put a $20 gold piece under each child's dinner plate. Anna saved hers. Years later she gave them all to Bishop Fulton J. Sheen.

"Wait until your father gets home," Catherine Murray would say. It was how she disciplined the children. When she gave them castor oil she put it in a small shot of whiskey. This, she thought, would keep them off the booze forever. They would be like their father. He never drank at all. The boys got an allowance of twenty-five cents a week; the girls got nothing. This was the way things were then in a respectable Irish Catholic home. A girl was not supposed to be touched by the things of the world; she was supposed to be above them. It was sanctified this way by the church and by God. Thomas Murray had a well-ordered Catholic home.

When the children were young, their grandfather Daniel Bradley lived with them. Honest Dan had retired from the burdens of the state senate, although he had not given up the flair that had gotten him there in the first place. One day, he took his grandchildren to Coney Island in a carriage and team, and on the way the carriage ran over a man's hat. It was a new straw hat, a boater, and the man who had worn it on that windy day stood on a corner, growing red with annoyance and saying bad things about the driver of the carriage. A crowd began to gather, and that was all an old Irish politician needed. Honest Dan stood up. "Gold I cannot give you," he began, "but let me offer you some good advice." The advice was that the man ought only to buy hats with strings that tied under the chin, but it took Honest Dan fifteen minutes to say so.

Thomas E. Murray, meanwhile, was building and inventing. Electricity was fine, a promise for the future, but it could never do what it was supposed to do unless there were bigger and better power plants. In 1904, Murray designed a powerhouse in the Williamsburg section of Brooklyn. It was for the Brooklyn Rapid Transit Company, and it had a capacity of 112,500 kilowatts. Then there were Waterside No. 1 and Waterside No. 2 on the East Side of Manhattan. There was the Hell Gate plant on 134th Street. Then, for the Chattanooga & Tennessee River Power Company, Murray designed a hydroelectric plant in Chattanooga. He did not enjoy the experience. "Never trust a man who parts his hair in the middle — or a Southerner," he said, and spent most of the rest of his life in Brooklyn.

He kept a notebook by his bed, and he had a workshop in the basement. He was filled with energy, and in time he would hold 1100 patents, second in number only to the great Edison. Murray would awaken at night with an idea, make notes, and then perhaps work out a few things in the basement. He had set up his own small organization of consulting engineers, and in the morning he would go there, turn the sketches over to a toolmaker, and then go on to his offices in the Edison Company. In the evening he would return and there, he hoped, would be his new invention. "I'm glad that I know nothing about chemistry," he once said. "Otherwise, I think I'd go crazy." He meant there was just so much he could carry around inside him and that if there were more it would be the end of him. It was not just the power stations he was thinking of; he was thinking of smaller things, too.

He designed copper radiators, electric switches and fuses, refrigerating systems, flywheels and axle housings. Moreover, the history of new products is that the entrepreneurs who put them on the market do not care as much about whether they are safe as they do about whether they simply work. In the fullness of his energy, Murray found ways to keep electricity from hurting people. He designed seals that could not be opened and switches that would really work. In a way, he made the American home safe for electricity, and as the years went on his creative genius grew. When the war broke out, the British army was using mortars that fired shells made from thirty-two pieces of metal. Murray discovered a new electric welding process and then found a way of making the shells from only two pieces of metal. The American War Department was skeptical, but Murray went ahead, equipped his own factory, and made the shells anyway. They worked, and the War Department bought them.

This was a stern man, full of conviction, and quite capable of scaring the hell out of anyone. One Sunday, he was called into his factory. It was an emergency and the workmen were called in, too. One of them, a carpenter called Cooke, showed up in his best suit. Concrete was being poured into a wooden form and it splattered, mostly over Cooke's new suit. Cooke began to swear. It was a rich, ripe swearing, the language of a connoisseur. "Mr. Cooke," Murray said evenly, "are you saying your prayers?" Cooke stopped swearing.

In a way, Murray's genius, like his morality, was born from

absolute conviction. It is the way most genius operates. The old power stations were limited by the capacity of their boilers. The fires in the boilers were built on bricks, and the pipes carrying the water that was to be heated were laid above the bricks. Murray reasoned that one could build a better boiler and therefore a bigger power station by putting the pipes all around the fire rather than just above it. Other engineers, however, said that it couldn't be done this way. They said that the fire would just go out. But Murray did it his way and built a boiler with pipes all around it into the new Waterside No. 1 plant.

On the day the boiler was to be fired up, Murray was at a meeting, far from Waterside No. 1. He was called to the phone, and a man from the power station said they were trying, but that they simply could not start the fire. Try again, Murray said. He hung up and went back into the meeting. The phone rang again, and this time the man at the other end had a true note of urgency. They had tried again, he said, and they had failed again. The fire was still unlit, the boiler was cold, and Waterside No. 1 was a failure. Murray pondered, and then majestically he said: "Have they opened the flue?"

They had not, of course, but when they did the fire began to burn. It kept burning, and henceforth the new kind of boiler would be known in the trade as the Murray Wall of Water.

Thomas E. Murray was different from other people; he saw things in other ways, more simply, and therefore more originally. It was the secret of his genius. For years, for example, engineers had been going through elaborate processes in putting ducts through concrete. A duct is nothing much, only a hole through which are placed pipes or wires, but the problem is that it is hard to put a hole through freshly poured concrete. It came up at a meeting of engineers and manufacturers once, and Murray said that they ought simply to put a rubber tube through the concrete and then pull it out when the concrete was hard. He said it would leave a nice-enough hole behind it. Impossible, the engineers and manufacturers said. They were all high-powered, well-educated types, while Murray was more or less unlettered. They said the rubber tube would stick in the concrete. They all knew that. "Gentlemen," Murray said, "I've been doing it this way for years." Then he picked up a rubber band from a desk, stretched it back and forth, and showed them how it could really work after all.

Indeed, Murray was showing all kinds of people what a poor Irish boy could do. In 1910, he received the Longworth Medal of the Franklin Institute in Philadelphia for his "system of safety devices and protective appliances for interior electric wiring," and in 1913 he received the gold medal of the American Museum of Safety. Georgetown University told him in 1918 that it would make him a Doctor of Laws, and he had wired back, "Accept with thanks the great honor conferred on me by university," and truly meant it. Eventually, other Catholic institutions honored him, too.

Thomas E. Murray was not exactly celebrated in his time, practical inventors such as himself seldom becoming celebrated, but he was known in the councils of the church, and he was to stay a child of the church, which all of his children, save one, would also do. There was always Murray's piety, and he was the chief supporter of St. Gregory's Church in Brooklyn from the time it was founded. Every morning he would go there for seven o'clock Mass, first making the Stations of the Cross and then praying at the shrine of St. Joseph. He contributed to Catholic charities, found his way onto all kinds of bishops' committees, and was little inclined to quarrel with the priesthood or its works. His daughters were forbidden to go out with Protestants, and he preferred that his sons not have much to do with them, either.

What he truly felt about Protestants he did not say, but in fact it was a wonderful joke on the classy Protestants because they couldn't bear the thought of their children mingling with Irish Catholics. The French Catholics, having a certain cachet, weren't bad. The German Catholics weren't much, and the Italian Catholics were unspeakable unless they were marquises from decaying Tuscany. The Irish Catholics were different from all of them. Irish Catholicism, everyone knew, was for the servants.

Consequently, the children of Thomas E. Murray moved in a small circle, like going to like, as people once said, family, church, and the children of the other rising Irish. Thomas Jr. was serious, intelligent, more like his father than any of the others. Even before Thomas E. Murray died, Thomas Jr. would be his surrogate, handling the other children in the family and inspiring very nearly the same feelings in them that the father did. Thomas Jr. would grow to be rich and celebrated, a member of the Atomic Energy Commission, often a possibility for this political office or that, and he would dwell in the halls of his God forever.

Joseph was outgoing, friendly, a joker. Once, Joseph led Tom Jr. into some improbable mischief, and an overwrought Irish policeman picked the boys up and took them to the station house. Honest Dan, brandishing a malacca cane, came down to get them out. Everyone liked Joe, and he would marry into money, marry the daughter of the president of U.S. Steel, in fact, and thereby become something of an example to his children. They would all marry money, too.

Daniel was bright, witty, full of charm, the one everyone assumed would be a success. Sometimes they thought of him as brilliant. Still, Daniel carried a darkness in him. What it was no one knew, but in a time to come, when he was living out his years in mental institutions, his brothers and sisters would scarcely mention his name. If they did, it would be to tell their children that he was dead.

John, the youngest boy, was vulnerable, too. His was a

darkness different from Daniel's, but a darkness just the same. He was perhaps more romantic, more hopeful, more expecting of good things than the others. Why not? When he was ten he had even invented a baseball game, something to be played on a board with strings and pulleys, and he had pleased his father. Thomas Murray had shown it to his attorney and they had had it patented. A year later he had shown it to Edison. The great man had taken the plans, and on them he had written: "This is pretty good for a boy only 11 years old to have invented. It's 'going some.' Edison."

John Murray would die when he was thirty-seven. He would go far in politics and business for one so young, although never as far as he wanted to, and he would be the saddest story of all. He would leave seven children and a wife who would never marry again. His daughters would be celebrated beauties, and one of them would marry Alfred Vanderbilt. And yet, John would still be the saddest story of all.

Then there were the daughters of Thomas Murray. Catherine was the best looking; everyone thought of her that way, and she would marry a man who was good looking, too. No one in the family was ever quite sure what he did, but they would say that he drank. They would adopt two children, and then they would separate. She, being what she was, would never ask for a divorce.

Anna was the strong one. She was always that way, and she was the only one who was never afraid of her father. One night, coming home from a date, she paused too long on the porch. When she walked in, Thomas Murray was furious. "Where the hell have you been?" he yelled. "Where the hell do you think I've been?" she said, and walked up the stairs.

Anna's strength would abide, and she would marry into the most money of all. Then one of her daughters would marry Henry Ford, and that daughter's daughter would marry Stavros Niarchos. Anna would live to see her church changed, the old verities and even her money gone. She would never seem to notice any of it, and the strength would abide.

Julia was terrified of her father, and sometimes she brooded over a family picture. She was the only girl in the picture whose dress did not have ribbons. It bothered her. She would marry a rich man, too.

Marie was the baby in the family. She was cosseted, pampered. She would be the one who was sent to finishing school. She would marry Anna's brother-in-law. It would be a poor marriage, but then he would die and she would marry again. To a Protestant. The family hardly ever saw her after that.

There was a ritual in the home of Thomas E. Murray. Before one of the girls went on a date, the father, the mother, the girl, and the date would say the rosary together. They would say it in the living room, and if they did not say it there they would say it in the hallway. If, God forbid, Catherine, Anna, Julia, or Marie slipped out of the house without saying it, Thomas Murray would follow them out onto the sidewalk. Sometimes he would catch up to them when they were already in an automobile, and he would lean through a window. "I believe in one God," he would say, and Catherine, Anna, Julia, or Marie would say it, too.

II

Propriety and Piety

THE OLD LEGEND is that every Irishman like Thomas E. Murray is descended from a king, and for once an old legend may be right, kings having once been so numerous in Ireland that it might be hard for an Irishman not to be descended from one. Old Ireland of the mists had some forty clans, and each one had a king, and above them all were a few more kings. The kings were elected, with no theological nonsense about divine right, which shows that even way back then the Irish had a talent for both politics and democracy. They were a Celtic people, who had come from somewhere out of northwest Europe centuries before the birth of Christ, and about them we do not know very much except that before they were driven out of Europe they had pretty much overrun it. Certain old Roman writers also tell us that these Celts were bombastic, belligerent, and sentimental, a terror to their enemies and a joy to their friends, and these, of course, are all things that people have been saying about the Irish ever since.

In fact, the Irish have mooned about and frequently said these things about themselves, sometimes forgetting that the sound most often heard out of Ireland was a wailing, a keening, or a long lamentation. One suspects that the Irish not only learned to live with suffering, but even to find a fierce joy in it. It is the unmentionable thing about Ireland, as it is about death and suffering in general, but without it the Irish might not have survived at all, and at the very least their music would have been different. So, in the very beginning there were the Celts and their kings, their bards and their Druids. (There were other people in Ireland before this, but they are lost in even deeper mists than the Celts.) The bards were poets with lyres, and the Druids were priests and philosophers, full of talk about their gods and the dark mysteries of Ireland.

This was an age of heroes, of Conor MacNessa, of Cuchullain, of Conn of the Hundred Battles, of Cormac, of Niall of the Nine Hostages. It was also an age of legend, and the legends persisted and survived, heartening 2000 years of Irishmen, and then moving to America, where they heartened some more. Fordham graduates who one day found their way onto the New York Stock Exchange would sometimes recite stories as legends without really knowing what it was that moved them to do it. It would be a romantic thing, and the impulse to do it would be the same as it had been with the bards.

Perhaps the greatest of all events in Irish history was the coming of St. Patrick in 432 A.D., which would have been the fourth year of the reign of Laoghaire, son of Niall, the high king. Actually, it may have been Patrick's second visit. He is supposed to have gone first to Ireland in the year 389 as a captive, taken in a raid on Brittany by King Niall's men, and then to have remained there as a shepherd until his escape seven years later. Whatever the chronology, for all practical purposes Patrick converted Ireland to Christianity, although it is almost certain that there had been Christians there before him. In the years before Patrick, for example, St. Jerome complained of one Celestius, an Irishman who argued doctrinal matters with him. Celestius, he said, was a "stupid fellow, loaded with the porridge of the Scots," by which he meant the Irish. Nonetheless, Christianity flourished, and in time Ireland was sending out missionaries to benighted Europe. It was the Celtic, or Gaelic, age, an age of glory for Ireland, and it began to decline when the invaders came. First, there were the Danes. They built the first Irish towns, the Irish having always been a people of the forests and fields, and then there were the Normans. The Danes were driven out by Brian Boru, the only man ever to unite all the Gaels in common cause, and the first and last true emperor the Irish ever had. His army won on Good Friday in 1014, although in that moment of triumph a Viking split his head with an ax. The other Irish kings waked Brian for twelve days, and then, of course, fell once more to fighting among themselves.

The Normans were something else. They had conquered England in 1066, and in 1169 their Henry II tried to conquer Ireland. He was helped by the treachery of Dermot MacMurrough, who was the King of Leinster, by Pope Adrian IV, who, before his death in 1159, talked about bringing Ireland back to a truer Christianity, and by an army of Welsh and Flemish archers. Still, Henry II never succeeded in conquering Ireland, and the other English kings of the next few centuries never did, either. By 1500, the English controlled only the Pale, that small area around and about Dublin, and the old Normans had disappeared into the Irish, with the Geraldines, for instance, becoming the Fitzgeralds, and the DeBurgos becoming the Burkes. Nevertheless, the Pale festered in Ireland, and Ireland began to wither. In 1366, the English had written the Statute of Kilkenny, a clearly racist law, which said that those who wished to remain in the Pale had to renounce all things Irish. They could not speak Gaelic. They could not wear Irish clothes, play Irish games, or even have Irish names. It was the price they were to pay for remaining under English law, and indeed outside the Pale there was little but anarchy. "There is no land in the world of so long continual war within himself," a paper of the English court said. "Ne of so great shedding of Christian blood, ne of so great robbing, spoiling, preying and burning, ne of so great wrongful extortion continually as Ireland." The dark time was coming down on Ireland, and the Gaelic age was disappearing, ready to be crushed by the captains of Elizabeth I.

It remained for Henry VIII to propose the final solution for Ireland: a religious war. Ireland would be colonized and her church erased. Pope Pius V took this so seriously that in 1570 he issued a papal bull saying that Elizabeth, Henry's daughter, had no right to rule either England or Ireland. The papal bull made no difference, but it did at once and for all time join the Catholic church and the destiny of Ireland. Not long afterward, Hugh O'Neill, Earl of Tyrone, who was the last of the great Gaelic chiefs, was leading the last of the great rebellions. He was from Ulster in the north, the final resting place of the Gaelic culture, and when he lost after nine years of war the Gaelic world died, too.

There were other rebellions, but by now it was nearly all over for Ireland as a nation. In the decade after Cromwell invaded Ireland, somewhere between one third and one half of the population died, not only of war, but of plague and famine, and that godly man became the first great modern practitioner of genocide. Still, Irish resistance flickered on, and in 1688 the Irish rallied to the dethroned James II. The Irish lost again, the Battle of the Boyne and the siege of Limerick being the great disasters, and by 1691 it was all over. Ireland was gutted, wiped out. The last of the Irish nobility fled, becoming the "Wild Geese" of new legends, and in time they and their descendants would do glorious deeds in the armies of other nations, although never again in Ireland's. Ireland was for beggars, and in the early 1700s, England, which already had confiscated most of the fertile land in Ireland, began to enact the worst of the Penal Laws.

It is simply no good trying to understand the Irish in America without knowing about the Penal Laws. They

shaped the Irish character and made resentment something the
Irish carried with them wherever they went. The American
Irish, even the most successful ones, still carry that resentment
with them. The other lasting heritage of the Penal Laws is
that they may have been greatly responsible for another enormous Irish American impulse: the urge for respectability.
After all, the Penal Laws, which shaped the mind of a race,
had supposed that there was no such person as an Irish Catholic, but that if there were it was someone of an order less than
human.

They had begun by saying that no Irish Catholic could have
a "gun, pistol or sword . . . under penalty of fine, imprison-
ment, pillory or public whipping," and then had gone on to
banish "all Popish Archbishops, Bishops, Vicars-General,
Deans, Jesuits, Monks, Friars and all other regular Popish
clergy" from Ireland. A priest who ignored the order could be
hanged, drawn, and quartered. At different times and at different places in Ireland the laws would be enforced with different
degrees of severity, but they would last until well into the
1800s, and they would be, as Montesquieu said, "written in
blood, and registered in Hell."

Under the Penal Laws, the Irish Catholic could not vote.
He could not hold office, enter a profession, or take part in
commerce. For a while, he was not supposed to live in a city,
or even within five miles of one. He could not own a horse
worth more than five pounds, and he could neither educate his
children himself, nor send them to a Catholic schoolmaster.
He could not purchase land, and he could not rent land that
was worth more than thirty shillings a year. Even with that,
he could not take from his land a profit of more than one third
of the rent, and if he did he would forfeit the land to the first
Protestant who informed on him. He could not really do anything except live and die and in between that starve. It was
the way things were in Ireland for a long time, and in 1776,

when a British peer asked his colleagues in the House of Lords to make it lawful for an Irish Catholic to lease a cabin and potato garden, he was called a "papist" and voted out of his chair.

The Penal Laws were a misery peculiar to the Irish, visited on them by the English, and they were followed by the Great Famine, a misery visited on them by nature. To be sure, there had always been famines. In 1741, for example, more than 400,000 persons died, and at the time of Cromwell even more than that had perished. But the famine that settled over Ireland in the late 1840s was the greatest tragedy of all. No one knows with any certainty how many died then of hunger and disease, and there are only speculations. In 1841, there were more than 8 million people in Ireland, but in 1851 there were only 6.5 million. It is figured that, at a normal rate of increase, the population in 1851 ought to have been 9 million; therefore, there was a loss of 2.5 million persons. About a million Irish emigrated in the late 1840s, and so it would seem that 1.5 million died in the famine. Whatever the number, the horror was unspeakable, and perhaps even more perished. Typhus spread. Hundreds of thousands of beggars tramped the roads. The poor sold all they had, and in the end they simply had nothing. They wore rags, and at night they slept under another pile of rags. Relief societies, unable to buy enough coffins to bury the dead, found they could make do with a single coffin with a hinged bottom. Sometimes there was not even that, and the bodies of the Irish just lay where they had died.

It was in this time of misery that the great migration began — to all parts of the world, but mostly to America, and in the beginning the migration, like the famine, was full of pain and sorrow. Few records were kept of the toll taken by the Atlantic voyages, but it is known that in the year 1847, 100,000 of the Irish sailed for Canada. It is thought that

17,000 of them died on their ships, the dreadful "coffin ships," that more than 20,000 died in Canada within a year of their arrival, and that at least 25,000 more had to go into hospitals. Grosse Isle, in the middle of the St. Lawrence River, thirty miles from Quebec, had been selected as a quarantine station for the Irish, and there is on Grosse Isle today a monument. On one side it says:

> IN THIS SECLUDED SPOT LIE THE MORTAL REMAINS
> OF 5,295 PERSONS, WHO, FLYING FROM PESTILENCE
> AND FAMINE IN IRELAND IN THE YEAR 1847,
> FOUND IN AMERICA BUT A GRAVE.

There were survivors, however, and many of them went to America. Sometimes they walked clear through New England, settling down here and there, leaving behind them small churches along the way. Some of them, like John Ford, a farmer from County Cork, chose the Midwest. His wife had died in Canada, and he had crossed the Great Lakes to Detroit, where he was to farm once again. He was the grandfather of that obsessive patriot Henry Ford, who began the automobile industry, and who, as these things were to go, was never thought of as being Irish.

From 1820 to 1840, about 700,000 Irish came to America. From 1840 to 1860, 1.7 million came, with the total steadily rising every year until 1851, when 216,000 Irish came to America. It had been terrible for them in Ireland, but for many it was almost a penance to leave. The early monks had a phrase for it. When they left Ireland to go into the reaches of the world they spoke of a "white martyrdom." It meant they were leaving their homes and everything they loved, and they said it was the gravest penance of all.

And what of the English, the lords of Ireland? In the famine years the British government had made some small efforts toward easing the Irish pain, but it had not done much, and even in the worst of the years Ireland still exported much of the little food it was producing. Why not? The famine was the work of God, and the great migration was an extra blessing. "They are going! They are going! The Irish are going with a vengeance," the London *Times* exulted in an editorial. "Soon a Celt will be as rare in Ireland as a Red Indian on the shores of Manhattan." Alfred Lord Tennyson, that master of Victorian sentiment, said it even better: "The Celts are all made furious fools. They live in a horrible island and have no history of their own worth the least notice. Could not anyone blow up that horrible little island with dynamite and carry it off in pieces — a long way off?"

Obviously, these Irish of the great migration were a despised people, with nothing but Ireland and blighted hopes to look back on, and possibly not very much to look forward to. One cannot measure these things, but it is probable that America welcomed them less than it has any other group of immigrants either before or since. Moreover, the Irish who had gotten here before the famine Irish weren't too sure of them, either. Bishop John Hughes of New York, a conservative and sometimes difficult man, was forthright about it. He called these new immigrants "the scattered debris of the Irish nation," with "a dangerous and bad class among them." He also observed that the adults among them died early on and easily, and this, he was sure, would lead to "the consequent dereliction of their numerous offspring." The Bishop thought that America ought to stop all emigration from Ireland for at least a decade.

Meanwhile, America itself was changing its ideas about the Irish, a process nicely reflected in the work of the famous cartoonist Thomas Nast. At midcentury he was drawing the Irishman as a simple drunken peasant, a clown without menace. Gradually, however, his Irishman changed. He became simian, prognathous, barely human, and, if you will, wicked. It was almost understandable. Having known a bucolic suffering for so long, the Irish elected to stay in the American cities, particularly New York. Even at its most generous, America has always been suspect of New York, and as early as 1850 New York was in danger of becoming an Irish city. About a quarter of the people there, 133,000 out of 513,000, had been born in Ireland, and if one considers their children and the other members of the second and third generations, then New York was more than one-third Irish.

There had always been Irish in New York, several hundred of them having swarmed into an old brewery to live as early as 1792, and there were even the beginnings of a respectable society among the Irish. On the eve of St. Patrick's Day in 1831, some of them held their first Erina Ball, thereby reminding the other New Yorkers that they were a people to be reckoned with, and at the same time reminding themselves that there were Irish and there were Irish, and that if you could get on a restricted guest list and afford an expensive ticket to a ball, then you might not be such a bad fellow after all. It was the Irish bourgeois way of confirming the contours of their own existence, and one way or another some of the Irish would always exclude the rest of the Irish from their own high society. "The Irish are a fair people," Samuel Johnson once said. "They never speak well of one another." Dr. Johnson was being witty, but there was something there to be considered. The Irish who had money did not look kindly on the Irish who did not, and indeed they hardly ever would through all the time they were in America.

In the 1840s, the Irish were filling up the old Five Points district of New York, making it a neighborhood known for its noxiousness, and shortly afterward they filled up the streets along the East River. These were slums, without sewers, without amenities, and the wonder is that anyone survived them. As it was, most of the Irish there and in the other slums just barely survived. The tuberculosis rate among the Irish in prosperous America was far higher than it had been in Ireland; so was the death rate from all causes. A higher proportion of the Irish than other immigrants went insane, especially young women, and the curse of alcohol, which the Irish called "the creature," became a thing of legend. Moreover, the Irish were filling up the poorhouses. From 1849 to 1891, about 60 percent of the inmates of the New York City Alms House were Irish, and the number went below that figure only twice in those years. In other cities it was much the same.

Worse, the Irish were getting themselves a reputation as lawbreakers, disturbers of the peace, and hooligans in general. In New York in 1859, more than half of those arrested were Irish. Their crimes were seldom serious, but the other Americans didn't notice that; it was enough that they were Irish. This was also an age of riots, and the Irish were involved in more than their share of them, sometimes as victims, but as often as not as the people who started them. "Scratch a convict or a pauper, and the chances are that you tickle the skin of an Irish Catholic," the Chicago *Post* said in 1869. George Templeton Strong, the uppity New York diarist, said of the Irish that "the gorilla is their superior in muscle and hardly their inferior in moral sense," and some of the Irish newspapers in America were scarcely less temperate than Mr. Strong. Their editorial writers regularly said that some of their fellow countrymen were "semi-barbarians" and a "disgrace to Ireland," and more in sorrow, Thomas D'Arcy McGee, the Irish intellectual, said the problem was that the Irish had not been taught "fundamental cleanliness, sobriety, caution, perseverance, or the other minor details."

With so much going against them, it is hard to see how the Irish got anywhere at all. They had been persecuted in Ireland, and now they were enjoying the poorest of reputations in America. Furthermore, they had few of their own to look up to. Here and there were a few authentic Irish aristocrats and millionaires, but they were not idols of the Irish crowd, and they wouldn't have enjoyed the roles much anyway. There were the heroes of various small uprisings against the English, who periodically fled Ireland and came to America, and in the Mexican and Civil wars there were those Irishmen who became celebrated on the battlefields. But these were fleeting glories, won by men whose skills did not easily transfer to the marketplace or the very best drawing rooms, and who might not have known what to do in the drawing rooms even if they had. There was John Morrisey, who had been born in Tipperary and brought to America as a boy, and who won the heavyweight championship in 1853. He went on to Congress, made a fortune, and founded a gambling hall in Saratoga Springs. The New York Irish loved him, and 15,000 of them followed the cortege to his grave. Later there was John L. Sullivan, but his drinking and his profession made him a raffish man, too.

There were Irish politicians, of course, but unfortunately the best-known among them were usually the most venal. There was, for example, Richard Croker, who became the boss of Tammany Hall in 1886, and who, having been born in County Cork, was always accepted as an authentic Irishman, even though he was descended from an English family that had only settled in Ireland. Croker stole with both hands, and eventually he bought both his own Pullman car and a mansion just off Fifth Avenue. When the forces of reform swept him from New York, he retreated to Ireland, bred thoroughbred horses, and on his death at the age of seventy-nine left $5 million to the young woman who was supposed to be his third wife.

One problem was that the Irish who came here had no tradition of business or commerce, and indeed in Ireland there had even been scorn for those with too keen an eye for money, or too much of a proclivity for making it. Certainly the Penal Laws and other misfortunes had prevented the Irish from going into business, but there was something in the Irish temperament besides. The Gaelic heroes had been warriors, priests, poets, and scholars, and latter-day Irish would dismiss the settlers the English brought into Ulster as "weavers, shop-keepers and merchants." Nearly all those few Catholic Irish in Ireland who did prosper in trade wanted their sons to do something else — to become lawyers, say, or priests, or, if it were at all possible, municipal officeholders. The mere piling up of money, the notion of grubbing about in old ledgers, did not much enchant the Irish, and if one were to make money then it ought to be done with a flair.

Few of the first- or second-generation Irish in America made a great deal of money, and for every Anthony Nicholas Brady or John Mackay, the mining millionaire, there were ten thousand Irishmen whose rises to prosperity were lifetime struggles, or had started with their fathers before them. For the most part, the Irish here began as laborers and then went on to the skilled trades, and by the time of the Civil War most of the foreign-born carpenters, masons, plasterers, and brick-layers in New York were Irish. Some of them became con-tractors and prospered, and their children prospered even more. John B. McDonald, for example, was brought here by his father. The father became a laborer, and then a foreman, and finally a contractor with connections in Tammany Hall. His son inherited the business and the connections and built long stretches of both railroads and the New York City sub-way. When he died in 1911, there was a funeral in St. Pat-rick's Cathedral, and the city stopped all the trains for two minutes.

There were other paths to success besides contracting, and one of them was transportation. More than one Irishman began working in a stable, and then bought a wagon, and eventually began a bus service. More than one began by run-ning a saloon, and then went into the liquor business, or per-haps real estate. The selling of liquor never had the oppro-brium among the Irish that it had among their neighbors, and it was estimated at one time in the last century that 2000 saloons in Lower Manhattan were run by the Irish.

By perhaps 1900, enough of the Irish had climbed into the middle and upper middle classes to move themselves and the other Irish out of the immigrant group and into something else. What it was, exactly, no one quite knew, least of all the Irish. Sometimes it was self-consciously American, full of patriotism and what were supposed to be the old American virtues, and once in a while it was every bit as much Irish, with touches of wit and laughter, a certain boisterousness, and a serious devotion to old Ireland itself. It puzzled the other Americans, and frequently it aroused their scorn. Sometimes, however, the great Irish yearning for respectability and gentility, a yearning that the rising Irish at the turn of the century were turning into a mania, only made the other Americans laugh, which may have been the unkindest cut of all. It was the time of the lace-curtain Irish, those solemn creatures filled with mingled feelings of rejection and defiance, and it was the stuff of which parody was made.

Once, Edward Harrigan and his partner, Tony Hart, had been made famous by their sentimental songs and plays about the Irish. There had been the Mulligan series, which were plays filled with honest, impulsive, generous Irishmen, and there had been songs like "Remember, Boy, You're Irish," "The Gallant 69th," and "Why Paddy's Always Poor." The Irish had loved them. Then, in 1890, Harrigan discovered something new: the social pretensions of the Irish. The play was *Reilly and the 400,* and the hit song in it was "Maggie Murphy's Home":

> There's an organ in the parlor, to give the house a
> tone
> And you're welcome every evening in Maggie Murphy's
> home.

The Ancient Order of Hibernians liked none of these things, and seized by both the desire to rid the country of the stage Irishman and the urge to proclaim their own new respectability, they began a boycott of the theaters that put on offensive performances. The Hibernians were absolutely serious, just as they would be a few years later when they excoriated the work of Synge and Yeats, and at a performance of something called *The Fatal Wedding* in Wilkes-Barre, Pennsylvania, an Irishman leaped to his feet. A servant girl had just drunk from a bottle of wine, and this, the Irishman shouted, was an insult to Irish womanhood. The manners and morals of the Protestant majority were passing through the prism of the Irish-Catholic experience, and they were making a strange reflection indeed. In 1898, the Paulist Fathers put up this notice for their Irish parishioners in New York:

All persons who do not regularly rent seats on an annual basis must pay at the door before each service for all masses except the 5 A.M. At the 6 and 7 A.M., there is a charge of 5 cents per person for each seat. At the 8, 9, 10 and 11 the charge will be double, or 10 cents per seat, per person. The proper way, then, for all such persons is to secure a ticket at the door, and present it to the usher, who will try to provide you with as good a seat as he can. Some may fancy that they may pay what they can, and sit where they please. Such a course upsets all our calculations and puts to great inconvenience our regular pewholders. This is not good form, to say the least. To take any seat one chooses without regard for the prearranged and deserving rights of others shows very bad manners. Yet some take a seat as coolly as if they were on a frozen pond in December. You can walk all over them with perfect safety. It has no affect. The effort to remove them is as great an effort as moving an iceberg.

The prices fixed for the various masses are fixed and firm. Eight cents and a large medal will not warrant the ticket seller to give you a 10 cent ticket. Yet, some have made such bargains . . . Neither is the ticket box a subtreasury for bent or mutilated coins, or to put notes of abuse about our right to charge for God's seats. Any person with any grievance of this sort can easily settle the matter of displeasure with the Rector of this Church . . .

This announcement is not made for the poor people. We know who they are, and they can worship for free, as long as we know them.

By the early 1900s, propriety and piety were settling in on the heirs of the old Gaelic culture with an iron grip, and it was in these years that the children of Thomas E. Murray were growing up.

III

Tom's Children

DANIEL BRADLEY was gone. He had come to this country in 1849 at the age of nineteen, and in the beginning he had received mail from Ireland that was addressed simply to "Daniel Bradley, Fornenst the Catholic Church, Brooklyn, USA." Fornenst, as any Irish postman knew, meant nearby, and Honest Dan was nearby a Catholic church until the end of his life. He was the Murrays' connection to all that had gone on in Ireland before them, and when he died, his great cloud of hair gone white, the three-wheel bicycle on which he had taken his stately exercise up and down St. Mark's Avenue long since put away, the bone and blood of the Irish connection died too, staying on only as the most residual of memories. Many years later, Daniel Bradley would be remembered this way: standing in the window of his son-in-law Thomas E. Murray's home, too frail to march any longer in the St. Patrick's Day parade, and instead waving at the children from St. Joseph's and St. John's orphanages as they marched along St. Mark's Avenue and waved at him. He had never really talked much about Ireland, other than saying that it had been a dreadful crossing of the Atlantic that had brought him from the place, and indeed the most sentimental of the legends about Ireland have always been put forth by Americans who have never been there. Daniel Bradley, however, was a practical man, who taught Sunday school and was without pomp, and had a sense of humor, too.

The torrent of life went on without him, and one by one the Murray children came of age. Daniel, the first-born, went to college, his father having selected the Jesuits of Georgetown as the most suitable instructors for him, and Daniel had triumphed. He had always triumphed. It was his way, the way of the brightest and friendliest child in the family, the child everyone had noticed first. Georgetown had been easy, and then there had been Georgetown Law School, and that had been just as easy. In fact, Daniel had already graduated first in his class when the melancholia settled down on him. At first, his parents thought, it wasn't much — his diet, perhaps, or a need for fresh air, or exercise. Freud was a neurologist then, just beginning to agitate Vienna, and a pious man like Thomas E. Murray could only lay the problem at the foot of the Cross. He did that, and then he took Daniel for a trip abroad. The sea air. A change of scenery. The spas. It did no good, and the melancholia grew deeper, and Daniel took to his bed for longer and longer periods of time, neither wanting, nor able, to resurrect himself. In the end, it became hopeless, and he was sent to a retreat in Connecticut. They could not do much for him there, either, but when he could no longer recognize anyone, and his anguish had grown so intense, and he clenched his fists so tightly that the nails dug into the palms, the doctors thought to pry open his fists and stuff cotton into them. It was really all, they said, that they could do.

Anna Murray's rite of passage came next, taking place at Allenhurst on the New Jersey shore. Allenhurst was a summer place, and among the New York Irish, the Irish who were without the means of Fortune Ryan, say, or of John Mackay's son Clarence, but who were rising nonetheless, it was the best of all places. There was nearby Deal, New Jersey, and there were the Thousand Islands and Far Rockaway, where the Murrays had also spent summers, but Allenhurst was something special. It had éclat. For one thing, one met only other Irish Catholic families there, and some of the families would bring their favorite priests with them. The priests would sit on the porch of the great wooden hotel at Allenhurst, lending a silent benediction to the place, and then they would stroll along the beach, the portlier ones sweating, their faces turning red above the Roman collars, and it was all a sure and visible sign that God was everywhere, even at a summer resort. Besides, Allenhurst had big houses along the beach, not the marble sepulchers of Newport, but honest, decent places fit for large families that had Irish chauffeurs and maids to worry about. It had a golf course, golf having been introduced into the tonier Southampton in 1890, and on soft, summer nights, in the middle of that Irish Catholic gemütlichkeit, it had the melodies of Victor Herbert, who, as everyone knew, had himself been born in Dublin.

It was, in fact, a remarkably suitable place to fall in love, and it was there in 1915 that Anna Murray met James McDonnell. He was a small, dapper man in silk monogrammed shirts, and he was a partner in the brokerage house of Byrnes & McDonnell. Wall Street had never been kind about accepting Irish Catholics, an unkindness that was to persist for years, and so the tougher Irish Catholics had set about forming their own brokerage houses. James McDonnell was a very tough man, and he formed McDonnell & Company in 1917, a year after he married Anna.

A month after that marriage, Joseph Murray, fair hair, blue eyes, the picture of his mother, everyone said, married Theresa Farrell. She was the daughter of James A. Farrell, an immigrant who had gotten as far as the fourth grade, and who had subsequently become the president of U.S. Steel. Then he founded the Farrell Steamship Company.

Meanwhile, Thomas E. Murray, Jr., Yale '11, was courting Marie Brady. Her father had owned J. N. Brady & Company, a department store in Lower Manhattan, and she had known the Murrays all her life. She had known Daniel first, Daniel being the one who waved at everyone, and then she and young Catherine Murray had become friends. When Marie was twelve, her parents had died and she had been sent to a Sacred Heart convent, drifting away from Brooklyn for a while, but staying near enough to spend the summer of 1916 in Allenhurst. She and Thomas E. Murray, Jr., got engaged that fall and married the next January.

Six months after that, Catherine, the pretty one, married John Ennis McQuail, an extravagantly handsome man with a waxed mustache and a dozen plans for getting rich, none of which would ever succeed. He was a big, gentle man, who dropped the name John in favor of the more distinguished Ennis, and who liked children. His wife cried on their wedding night, and early on Ennis developed an affliction: he drank.

In June of 1918, Julia, the shy one, announced her engagement to Lester Cuddihy. His father published the *Literary Digest,* and he himself had graduated from Lawrenceville and Princeton and at the age of twenty-six was making a handsome salary in advertising. Lester was a sprightly man, with approximately the configuration of a good jockey, and he had announced his love for Julia at their first meeting. Thomas E. Murray did not particularly care for Lester, and he said he was a whippersnapper. Julia's brother John would take Julia into Manhattan so that she could meet Lester secretly, and on the day that Lester asked for her hand, he had to sprint after Murray, who was on his way to church and, as always, running.

Soon it was the fall of 1918, a time that would be solemnized in America by war and the end of war, and a time that would be solemnized among the Murrays by young John Murray's announcement that he, too, was married. In fact, he said, he had been married five months. John was nineteen; so was his bride, and he had been so apprehensive of telling Thomas E. Murray about the marriage that he had asked Lester Cuddihy to do it. "I can't," Lester said, "I'm having my own problems." Consequently, John told his parents himself. His bride, he said, was terribly nice. He had met her first on a blind date, but they had not gotten along, and in fact they had quarreled. Then, John said, he met her a year later at a party, a party he had gone to with a mortician's daughter, and they had fallen in love. They had eloped to St. Peter and St. Paul's Church in Hoboken, and they were, he said, terribly happy. He said she was so good looking that she had modeled for Howard Chandler Christy, and that her name was Jeanne Durand. The other thing John said was that he wasn't sure who her parents were, and that she was pregnant.

It is not really enough to know that the Murrays were shaken by John's announcement; it is more accurate to say that it reverberated through a couple of generations of that family, shaping children in ways they would only vaguely perceive and sometimes not even know, and that at the very least it was not what the upright and Irish Murrays expected of their youngest son. Still, in the beginning, the family did rally round. Thomas Murray insisted that John, whom everyone called Jack, buy Jeanne a wedding ring. He even gave him the money for it, and Tom's wife made small cries of welcome for Jack and Jeanne. Jack, it was decided, would remain at Stevens Tech, getting his degree, and then joining his father and brothers in the Murray Manufacturing Company. His wife would become part of the family.

No one really recalls now how the breach began, and at first it was imperceptible — small hurts, imagined slights, perhaps a feeling by Jack's brothers and sisters that Jeanne somehow had led him astray. The family had pitied and prayed over Daniel, and then entrusted him to doctors. Obviously, Jack was not like Daniel, but he was moody, unpredictable, suffering from time to time with an acute stammer and a hideous claustrophobia, and most certainly a lack of good sense. After all, he had sneaked off and gotten married before he even had a job, and he had married someone the family didn't know. Jack, it was clear, needed watching.

Meanwhile, life unfolded for the family. Thomas E. Murray, Jr., and his wife, Marie, moved into a house on St. Mark's Avenue that was just across the street from the older Murrays, and they began to raise the first of what would be their eleven children. They also began to visit the older Murrays in the evenings, and they did it so regularly that it became a ritual, sanctified by time. If they were not across the street by 8:00 P.M. their phone would ring, and when they answered they would hear the inventor's impatient voice. "Well?" he would say, and within minutes Thomas Jr. and Marie would be there, the son immediately retreating to his father's study, his wife going upstairs to talk to her mother-in-law and eat salt-water taffy. If Tom and Marie wanted to go to a theater at night they would always buy four tickets, and the older Murrays would go with them. It was something that was simply understood.

Soon, Marie, the youngest of the inventor's daughters, married John McDonnell, a brother of James, the husband of Anna. Everyone in the family suspected they weren't happy.

Joseph Murray and Theresa moved into a fine old home on Atlantic Avenue in Brooklyn and filled it with servants and other expensive things. Joe Murray always signed his name J. B. Murray, making small circles of the dots after the initials, and once a Railway Express man, arriving with a trunk, wanted to know if a Jo Bo Murray-io lived there. In the family, Joe was forever after called Jo Bo Murray-io, which he never minded at all. He was a malleable man, content to listen to his father and his brother Thomas Jr., and he was happiest in his garden, puttering with ivy. No one knew why

Joe thought his right hand was covered with germs, or why he would hold a cup or glass only in his left hand. Perhaps no one even thought about it.

Anna and James McDonnell, meanwhile, were beginning an upward trek that would lead them and their fourteen children in the depths of the Depression into a life and an apartment on Fifth Avenue that was only a little less magnificent than Blenheim Palace. First, however, they moved to Rye, New York, where they advertised for a chauffeur. They got one Tom Langtree, who appeared in puttees, walking up their drive, experienced by years of service on the Jay Gould estate. Young Jim McDonnell, the first-born son, turned a hose on him. Langtree turned it back on young Jim. "I don't think I need to interview you, Tom," Anna McDonnell said approvingly. He was with them for years.

When the McDonnells moved, Lester Cuddihy made jokes, saying that he wondered how James could ever carry all those bags of money with him. Then, someone in the family began to call James McDonnell "Little Caesar." The name stuck. By now, Lester and Julia were living in Manhattan and raising their children. "When your husband puts on his hat to go, you get up and go, too," Julia's mother-in-law once advised her, and shy Julia had taken this to heart, wandering just about everywhere with Lester except the Players Club, where women weren't allowed. "Never argue with your husband about little things," Julia would say, and in her home she would extend an ashtray, ready to catch the ashes from Lester's cigarette. Sometimes when the Cuddihys sat down to dinner, Lester would grandly send back whatever the cook had prepared and insist that only scrambled eggs, say, or a cheese sandwich would please him. Julia would see that Lester got scrambled eggs. Lester would talk about "hipper dippers," by which he meant jewelry, and when the stock market went up he would load it on Julia. Once, just for the hell of it, he decided to buy her some coats. One was ermine, one was red velvet and silver fox, and one was black velvet and more ermine. People said that Lester was a card.

Thomas E. Murray, meanwhile, was rushing through his last years the same way he had rushed through the first ones. There had always been a kind of imperiousness about him, a disdain for the things that bound other men, and when Washington imposed Prohibition, saying that henceforth he could not drink, he insisted that he damn well would drink, even though he had been an abstainer all his life. He sent Raymond, his dignified, white-haired butler out for a bottle, and when Raymond returned with some bourbon, Murray tasted it, spat it out, and wondered what anyone saw in the stuff anyway. But, as a matter of principle, he would keep liquor in the house from that moment until he died. To everyone's surprise, Murray found time for diversions as he grew older, even engaging the man who directed St. Cecelia's choir to give him singing lessons, and discovering that best of all he liked Irish songs. No matter, there was still nothing he loved to do more than work, and in his bedroom there was a bell that was connected to a Con Ed powerhouse. When something went wrong it rang.

Anthony Nicholas Brady, his old patron, had died in 1913, and was mourned on the obituary pages as one of the men who had made America great. Before his death, he had entrusted his sons to Murray, and Murray had taught them what he knew about a public utility. Then, after Brady died, one of the sons, young Nick Brady, began to take over his father's business interests. He and Thomas Murray, along with Murray's sons Tom Jr. and Joe, even became partners in something called the Metropolitan Device Company. The partnership did not last long, however, and neither did the friendship. Murray and Nick Brady fell out. Worse, Brady now wanted Murray out of Con Edison, too. "Next he'll want me to punch a time clock," Murray would say bitterly, and think of how he had commuted from Albany, and of how he had virtually built Con Ed with his bare hands. He told Tom and Joe to buy out Nick Brady's interest in the Metropolitan Device Company, and they did. It was a private deal, just the two of them, and they divided up Brady's shares among themselves. Later, when Thomas Murray died, his son Jack said that Brady's shares should have ended up in his father's estate. He wanted to bring suit over it.

As always among the Murrays, it was understood that after church on Sunday everyone would gather at Thomas Murray's house for dinner. It was a convention, as immutable as the one about going to Mass every morning. Consequently, it was a treachery to the family when the McDonnells missed some of the Sunday dinners because they were spending the time with Nick Brady and his wife. Brady, after all, was the inventor's enemy, conspiring to throw him out of Con Ed. It was unthinkable that the McDonnells should join him in his more affluent world, but they did, at least from time to time, and then they would be back again for Sundays at St. Mark's Avenue. Sometimes, Joe's wife, Theresa, would miss the Sunday dinners, too. Theresa had been raised with wealth; yet her mother-in-law would go on at length at the dinner table, talking about what was proper and what was not, and about how much she had learned by visiting the houses of elegant people. Theresa thought it was boring.

On most Sundays, however, all the Murrays would be there, and always there would be roast beef, just as there had been that night at General Talcott's years before. Jeanne, Jack's wife, hated the dinners. She rather liked Jack's father, but his mother was something else. The old lady looked down on her, Jeanne thought, not finding her quite respectable enough, or perhaps not enough of a Catholic. When Mrs. Murray and her daughters Anna and Catherine and her daughter-in-law

Marie lunched together at Maillard's on Madison Avenue, which they frequently did, Jeanne was not invited. It was a small wound, but it hurt. Jack, meanwhile, was growing closer to Lester Cuddihy and Ennis McQuail, finding them more companionable than Tom or Joe or the upright James McDonnell. It was a matter of style. True, Jack could be moody, but more often than not he was a sunny man, full of bonhomie, a cheerful irreverence, and an enormous capacity for making friends. There was a bit of glitter about Jack; he was something of a sport. Lester and Ennis were sports, too. Tom, Joe, and James McDonnell were not.

In 1927, Thomas E. Murray's wife fell into a final illness. Her departure, peaceful and in bed, was attended by family and friends, and across the street in the home of Thomas E. Murray, Jr., by a small fire set by her grandchildren. They had been praying, kneeling before votive candles and asking God's blessing on Grandma, when Jimmy, who was seven, got to wondering if tissue paper would burn. He touched it to the candles and it did burn, and then some curtains and bed-spreads burned, too. Marie Murray, who was eight, filled a potty with water and flung it about, and her brother Tommy, who was nine, ran naked and yelling from his bathtub. Miss Wiederman, the German nurse whom all the children disliked, swept in, threw the curtains and bedspreads out the window, and burned her hand. No one, however, could figure out how to work the fire extinguisher until the Irish chauffeurs, parked across the street outside the older Murrays', hurried over, ran upstairs, and used it to put out the rest of the fire. Miss Wiederman, her face puckered into martyrdom, walked around for days after that with a huge bandage on her hand. The children disliked her then more than ever.

Murray, three pairs of rosary beads at his side, died two years later in 1929. He was a Knight of Malta and a Knight of St. Gregory, and in the last year of his life, the Right Rev-

erend Thomas E. Molloy, Bishop of the Brooklyn Diocese, had
persuaded Rome to allow Thomas E. Murray to have a private chapel in his home. It was an honor given only to those
who loved God while showing success in dealing with Caesar,
and it was given to few, although one of them would be Nick
Brady, who one day would house his chapel in a mansion.
Murray was buried after a solemn Requiem Mass at St. Gregory's with not only Bishop Molloy in attendance, but fifteen
monsignors and seventy priests, too. "He was simple, sincere
and devoted to duty," the Bishop said in his eulogy. "He
shunned vulgar and inane ostentation. He was a stranger to
pretense and insincerity." So many people showed up for the
funeral that the police had to put on extra men to handle the
traffic, and the people who were unable to get inside St. Gregory's formed a crowd outside.

About 2000 people did get in, however, and among the
pews full of priests and other religious were pews full of Irish
Catholics who one way or another had made it in New York.
Al Smith was there, and so was Mayor James J. Walker.
There were also commissioners, aldermen, judges, and goodly
numbers of the merely rich. James A. Farrell, the president of
U.S. Steel, sat near William F. Kenny, the builder, who sat
near Barron Collier, the advertising man, who was a row from
Nicholas Brady. Thomas Edison sent a telegram saying he
was ill, and Samuel Insull, the utilities giant, sent his respects
from Chicago. When the Mass was over, Murray's coffin was
carried out between rows of orphans, the little boys in blue
uniforms, the little girls in white veils, and taken to Calvary
Cemetery in Queens. It was wonderfully Irish Catholic, this
passage of a good man from Brooklyn to Heaven, and a Catholic newspaper said earnestly that Murray had been "the leading and most representative Catholic layman in this large
diocese."

Thomas E. Murray had also been a patriarch, who was

leaving eight children and by the year of his death thirty-seven grandchildren, the oldest of whom was eleven. Murray's estate was worth about $9 million, which was not great wealth, but which was respectable enough for someone who had always been more involved with his work and his God than with his treasure. Within months of the funeral, however, the stock market crashed, and the estate was worth only $3 million. Actually, this scarcely mattered since all the children except the hospitalized Daniel were prospering. Even Jack was prospering, although he didn't know it himself. He had been associated with his father and brother in the family enterprises, but as the youngest son he had never really run any of them. There had been his father over all of it, and next to his father there had been his brother Tom, and next to Tom there had been his brother Joe. Jack had hated it. He had given most of his time to the Murray Radiatior Company, while being enough of his father's son to patent some inventions for Murray Conduit Systems. He had still hated it. In his soul he wanted to enter politics, where he could be a man among men and enjoy the feeling of power. The power might not truly be there, but this would hardly matter. It is the appearance of power that is so satisfying, and it is through the appearance of power that important Irish politicians have always run less important ones. Jack fitted into politics nicely.

Early on, he had joined a Democratic club in Brooklyn, and he had made friends. After Franklin Delano Roosevelt was elected Governor of New York in 1928, he appointed Jack Murray a commissioner of the Port Authority of New York. Jack was a stocky man, a little short of portly, and as a very young man he had grown a mustache, just as his father had before him, to make him look older. It pleased him to be a commissioner. He was full of plans. Thomas E. Murray, Jr., was drifting over into public life, too, although he would never quite do it with Jack's grace. Along with a former judge, Tom became the receiver for the bankrupt Interborough Rapid Transit Company. Sternly he began to guide it back to health.

Jack, meanwhile, decided to forsake the Murray family enterprises. They confined him, he said, scarcely allowing him the room or the opportunity to become the man he ought to become. Besides, they were too much of a family thing. It is difficult enough to be the youngest son in any large family; it was even harder in the Irish Catholic Murrays. They had a hierarchy, and Jack was at the bottom; everything came down on him. Jack wanted to get out, and he chose Wall Street. A man could make money there, he said, and in the 1920s even the least of men on Wall Street were making money. After his father's death, Jack bought a seat on the Stock Exchange for $250,000, but by now it was 1930. The great days of Wall Street were over, at least for a while, and things couldn't possibly work out for Jack as well as he hoped. He began to drink, not a lot, but a man who had been born with a bad liver ought not to drink at all. Not many people would ever see him drunk; he was better than that, but he kept a medicine bottle with Scotch in it when he was on the floor of the Stock Exchange, and sometimes he would sneak off to the bathroom for a belt. A doctor told him that if he did not stop he would be dead in five years. Jack said he was an alarmist.

He was a type, really, this youngest son of a prominent Irish Catholic family, and his reach would always exceed his grasp. He carried baggage of which he was hardly aware, and he was visited by most of the burdens and few of the consolations of a thousand years of Irish Catholicism. His brothers and sisters had the church, but Jack was skeptical of all that. They had one another, too, but Jack was closer to outsiders. He felt guilty about drifting from church and family; what Irish Catholic then would not? When someone suggested that he see Jung, who was visiting America, Jack laughed. Probably he was embarrassed. Jack went on, taking a drink when he was not supposed to, living elegantly, shopping at Sulka, and once even buying a Rolls-Royce when the market went up. But of course there would never be enough money for all the good things he thought he ought to have, and his brothers Tom and Joe and most of all his brother-in-law James McDonnell would always have more.

The McDonnells had forsaken Rye and moved to Manhattan. They did not take any old apartment, however; they moved to Fifth Avenue and 72nd Street into a simplex connected to a duplex, and it was supposed to be the largest apartment in New York. It had, for example, two kitchens, one for the youngest McDonnell children and the lesser members of the household staff, and the other for all the rest of the McDonnells and their staff. James, Anna, seven young McDonnells, and a cook, kitchen maid, butler, waitress, parlor maid, and chambermaid lived on one floor, and seven younger McDonnells and everyone else on the floor below. There was always a trained nurse, and over the years many, many governesses, the McDonnell children being such hell on them that they came and went with great regularity. Once, a governess was moved to call the police when a young McDonnell pursued her with an air rifle, and another time a young McDonnell, artfully moving a row boat away from a dock, managed to dump his governess into the lake in Central Park.

There was a rite of passage among the McDonnells: when a child on the top floor went off to school, got married, or otherwise moved away, a child on the lower floor moved up to take his place. Actually, a child could hardly tell the difference in floors. Everything, as one who had fallen in estate said years later, was very grand everywhere. The little McDonnell boys got their coats from Rowe's in London, and the little McDonnell girls got their underwear from an expatriate Russian princess. They all traveled, of course, and once they were in a restaurant in Belfast when two bishops walked in. Anna and

James had the children on their knees in an instant. In Paris they stayed at the George V, where a young McDonnell dropped a bag of water from the balcony above on the head of a fashion model below, and in London they stayed at the Grosvenor, where none of the children did anything worse than allow the tub to overflow.

Then, there was home to return to, and home was a place of perfect safety. Anna and James were always together, the one seldom being seen without the other, and around them there was all that money and sanctity, too. Anna was a daily communicant, and James very nearly so, and the Pope's picture hung in the living room. The children were seated at the dining table according to age, and once a week the hairdresser came up, first to do Anna and then to do the older girls. Everything was regular, well-ordered, and proper, and the McDonnells knew they were as good as anyone else. It was odd, really, the way some of them noticed Mrs. Twombly. Florence Twombly, herself a Vanderbilt, lived at 71st Street and Park Avenue, where her staff wore livery. Once, when young Jim McDonnell came home from school on vacation, he rented a suit of livery and then asked Tom Langtree to drive past Mrs. Twombly's house. Langtree was willing, and he took young Jim, all in livery, in the McDonnell car, past Mrs. Twombly's. She was, they thought, impressed.

Langtree, in fact, was an accomplice in much of what the young McDonnells did. He would take them sliding in the snow on Riverside Drive, and never tell Anna and James, who wouldn't have stood for it. Anna had once played on a coal pile in Albany, and James had gone swimming in the East River, but they wanted something else for their children, and Riverside Drive certainly wasn't it. The McDonnells, after all, were moving in the small proper world of the rich Irish Catholics of New York, and there were rules that had to be followed.

It is not true that the Catholic tradition in these families was handed down by the fathers; it was all done by the mothers. There was no one these ladies liked so much as a priest, and it was on a trip to Lourdes that Anna discovered Fulton Sheen. Actually, in the time before he became celebrated, wealthy Irish Catholics were always discovering Fulton Sheen. The first one to do it was apparently Thomas F. Farrell, who made his money in coal and iron, and then met Sheen as a very young man. Farrell helped pay for Sheen's education at the University of Louvain in Belgium and Sheen had gone on to greater things, three of them being the national director of the Society for the Propagation of the Faith, a radio and television personality, and a famous proselytizer of other famous people. One of them would be Henry Ford II, who, besotted with love, would marry Anne McDonnell, a daughter of Anna and James.

Anna's closest ally in the family was her brother Tom. Tom never missed daily Mass, either, and the joke in the family was that he had two living rooms in his house, one for Catholics and the other for everyone else. Certainly he was unhappy when his children brought home Protestants, but when he spoke about it at all it was only to point out rather primly that the most innocent relationships could lead to later, more dangerous, liaisons. In his world, he was right. When his son Tommy wanted to marry a Protestant girl, Thomas E. Murray, Jr., took him for an automobile ride. Tommy, he said, the marriage will never work. The girl was from a prominent-enough family, with an old Dutch connection that Thomas E. Murray, Sr., had known about when he was only a lamplighter in Albany, but she was still a Protestant. Furthermore, Thomas E. Murray, Jr., went on, when a man marries he just doesn't marry a woman, he marries into a family, and this family would never do. Young Tommy did not marry the girl.

The faith was everything to Thomas E. Murray, Jr., and always, it seemed, there were priests in his house. His children were raised with them, and for the most part they were not the kind who, thirsting for camaraderie, would take off their Roman collars and discreetly carouse. There were priests who played with the children, went on hayrides with them, and had a great fondness for golf, but they were never less than sacerdotal, at least when Thomas E. Murray, Jr., was around. If he was to be unbending in his faith and demeanor, they would be, too, and when a particularly eminent member of the clergy sat at his dinner table, Thomas E. Murray, Jr., would fall into a shy and respectful silence. For that matter, whenever Bishop Molloy visited Thomas Murray and his wife in their Southampton mansion they would unhesitatingly give up their bedroom to that notable divine, and then declare themselves fortunate for having had the privilege.

This was the way one lived, or was supposed to live, and it towered over everything else. When Joseph and Theresa Farrell Murray announced that their daughter Rosamund would marry Buckley Byers, there was a dilemma. Byers was a nice man, from what was called a good family, and he was obviously in love. Still, he was a Protestant. He agreed, however, to take instructions in the faith, to raise his children as Catholics, and to do very nearly anything else the family asked except to become a Catholic himself. He and his bride were to be married in Joseph and Theresa Murray's house on East 90th Street, and Monsignor Coleman Nevils, the president of Georgetown University, was to unite them. The boys' choir from St. Ignatius Loyola would sing, and the ceremony would be performed in a movable chapel that was to be carried down from the Farrell house in Connecticut. Joe Murray had extra pews built for it, and on the day of the wedding the house looked almost like a church. There were French tapestries on the wall, lilies banked everywhere, and the monsignor and the boys' choir were all in red. Thomas E. Murray, Jr., missed it. His car had broken down, he said, and he was able to get there only for the reception. Hardly anyone believed him, of course, and years later he would admit that he simply had been unable to attend the ceremony. "If I had gone," he was to say, "I would have signified my approval to my children." Tom Murray would make millions, become a member of the Atomic Energy Commission, and be discussed as a candidate for the Senate. The faith would still be what counted.

IV

Grandees and Climbers

BEING IRISH, the Murrays and McDonnells did not roam in the very best reaches of society, the very best reaches being filled up with those who could trace their eminence back at least a generation or so before they could. There was something called café society, but this was not the authentic article, lacking the class that real society was supposed to have and filled with people who didn't necessarily have any eminence at all. Younger Murrays and McDonnells would be big in it, but the older Murrays and McDonnells, caught up in that period when the Irish were only moving out of the immigrant class and propriety still counted, would spend their time mostly with one another. It was not always this way for the Irish Catholics, and in the beginnings of this country, no matter how distasteful Catholicism was to everyone else, there were Irish Catholics even among the exquisites.

The greatest one of all, probably the richest man in early America, in fact, was Charles Carroll of Carrollton, an ascetic grandee, who signed the Declaration of Independence and left behind him when he died an estate of 80,000 acres and a daughter who was the first grande dame of American society. The very first Carroll in this country, who was also called Charles, had come to Maryland in 1688 as the attorney general to the third Baron Baltimore. The Catholic James II was king then, his short reign ending in what the English called the

Glorious Revolution, and he was replaced by his Protestant son-in-law, William of Orange. William revoked Baltimore's charter, made Maryland a crown colony, and saw to it that the Assembly there established the Church of England as the official and only House of God. Actually, only about 10 percent of the Maryland colonists were Catholic, but the Assembly was implacable about them, and so the Catholics were reduced in their liberties to approximately the condition of the Catholics in Ireland. They could not vote, hold office, or, among other things, even educate their children as Catholics. The capital of Maryland was moved from St. Mary's City to Protestant Annapolis, and the old chapel at St. Mary's was torn down, erasing the last tangible reminder of Rome from what was now Puritan soil.

Still, the Maryland Catholics were not totally deprived. Most importantly, they could make money and that, of course, has always been the sine qua non for the building of any great family. Charles Carroll made a fortune in land and tobacco, and he did it while never straying from his faith, which other distinguished men sometimes did easily. In 1713, for example, the fourth Baron Baltimore, hopeful of regaining his family's old proprietary rights over Maryland, announced his conversion to Anglicanism. He died two years later.

The second Charles Carroll, called Charles Carroll of Annapolis, increased his father's estate and prospered, becoming possibly the richest man in the colonies. "We derive our descent from princes," he once wrote, "and until the Revolution [of 1688], notwithstanding our sufferings under Elizabeth and Cromwell, we were in affluent circumstances and respected." This, however, may not have been absolutely accurate. As respected as they may have been, the Carrolls had come down only from the O'Carrolls, who had been blessed merely with a large amount of property and probably no title at all. As a Catholic, wealthy as he was, Charles Carroll of Annapolis could still not take part in public life, or even in open worship in church. Furthermore, nearly any child in Maryland might trip along to a chant like this:

> Abhor that arrant whore of Rome
> And all her blasphemies,
> And drink not of her cursed cup,
> Obey not her decrees.

It left Charles Carroll of Annapolis a sour man, although his son, Charles Carroll of Carrollton, was different. "We remember and forgive," he said, and indeed he forgave the country every injustice that had been committed against him. As a boy he had gone to Europe for his education because Maryland law would not allow him to be taught by other Catholics, but as a man he became a delegate to the Continental Congress, and then helped to run the war. In 1792, in fact, the Federalists were ready to nominate him for the presidency if George Washington declined a second term. Washington did not decline and so Charles Carroll eventually returned to Carrollton, where he allowed the world to wait on him.

In his nineties, long after it was fashionable, he wore gold buckles on his shoes and lace ruffles at his wrists and along his shirtfront. He took a cold bath every morning, rode ten miles a day, and other than a glass or two of Madeira, champagne, or claret he drank not at all. He read books, went to bed at nine, and got up at dawn. When he died in 1832 at the age of ninety-five, he was a national monument and the kind of patrician neither the Irish nor the country would ever see again.

His daughter, Mrs. Richard Caton, was pushier. She set out to conquer society, and she did, becoming the first American matron to recognize the worth of having a European title in the family and subsequently marrying off her three daughters to English peers. One daughter became the Duchess of Leeds, another the Baroness Stafford, and the third the Marchioness of Wellesley. In London, they were called "the American graces." Then, Mrs. Caton helped to establish America's first great social resort. It was at White Sulphur Springs in Virginia, and it was presided over by a Mr. Caldwell, who was a despotic old party with white hair that he tied in a little queue. Even then the rich loved to be bullied, and so Mr. Caldwell took into his hotel and cabins only those people he knew, or whose family he had heard of, and who traveled in private carriages. He charged them $8 a week, and when Mrs. Caton began to spend the season there, it became the toniest place in America.

In New York, meanwhile, there was Dominick Lynch, who years later would be called by Ward McAllister "the greatest swell and beau" the city had ever known. McAllister, who proposed the names for the famous "400," would say that his career had been inspired by Lynch's, although in truth Lynch was a man of substance, while McAllister was not. Lynch was the favored son of old Dominick Lynch, who came from Galway before the Revolution, made a fortune in shipping, and was referred to by George Washington as "the handsome Irishman."

Within a few generations, almost all the Lynches would drop away from the church, but in the beginning, at least, they were devout. One of old Dominick's sons became president of the Utica Insurance Company, and another married the daughter of a prominent Irish liquor dealer, and the third was young Dominick Lynch. He was a wine importer, and he built a mansion in Westchester that was distinguished by a Carrara marble fireplace, and a town house at No. 1 Greenwich Street. Socially, Lynch was considered brilliant, with charm, good manners, and an authentic devotion to music. Once, he went to London, got together an opera troupe, and then brought it over on a packet ship. It was the first time New York had ever been exposed to grand opera, and Lynch helped to coach the company in *The Barber of Seville,* which it performed at the Park Theater in 1825. An ex-king, Joseph Bonaparte, was in the audience, and besides him, the *Evening Post* said, "an assemblage of ladies so fashionable, so numerous, & so elegantly dressed." Emboldened, Lynch and his friends subscribed $6000 apiece for boxes to start the Italian Opera House. New York, however, wasn't quite ready for it, and it went bankrupt after two seasons.

Lynch died from dropsy in Paris in 1837, and when he did the diarist Philip Hone mourned him as the most sought after man of his generation, and a speaker at the New-York Historical Society said he was "the acknowledged head of the fashionable and festive board, a gentleman of the *ton."* No one knew it at the time, but he would also be the last Irish Catholic to be thought of this way for many years. Socially, at least in the East, the Irish had run out of time. The canal workers and their brothers were descending, stamping a picture of Irish lowlife on polite American sensibilities and impeding for generations to come the progress of any other Irishman into the *ton* of Lynch or Carroll.

In the West, however, it was different. It had no *ton* to begin with, and it was freer, more open, and eager to put forth its own aristocracy. Some of the Irish who went there became bankers, builders, kings of gold and silver, and finally some of the great social climbers of all time. They did these things with wit, courage, and sometimes consummate silliness, and all the while they were no different from thousands of Irish laborers, draymen, and chambermaids in the East. The West, so far as the Irish rich were concerned, was the true melting pot of the last century, and San Francisco was the greatest melting pot of all. San Francisco never suffered through a mauve decade. Scattered about on seven times seven sand hills, it was a wilderness one day and a boisterous city the next. The Irish liked it. One of the first to settle there was Don Timoteo Murphy, who got a land grant near San Rafael in 1828, when California was still a part of Mexico, and raised cattle and Irish greyhounds. Murphy remained long enough to make friends with Jasper O'Farrell, who one day would lay out the city of San Francisco. Together they made the first public donation for charity in the city's history, a plot of ground for an orphan asylum.

In the beginning, San Francisco was only a village, and when American rule came to it in 1847 it had a population of 450, which included 34 Italians, 40 Hawaiians, and, apparently, 14 people who had been born in Ireland. Gold was discovered in 1848, and the year after that 700 shiploads of people disembarked at what was still a town without houses, raising the population from 2000 at the beginning of the year to 20,000 at the end. One of those who came was Peter Donahue. He had been born of Irish parents in Glasgow in 1822, and as a young man he struck out first for New York and then for the goldfields. Finding no gold, he became first a blacksmith and boilermaker, and then he formed a company to light the city with gas. He found money to import pipes from the East and coal from Wales, and subsequently gave San Francisco its first streetlights. He ran a steamship line between the city and Sacramento and built the first street railroad in California and the first iron foundry, too. He also put up a mansion, and once in a moment of whimsy he gave his wife a coach made entirely of glass.

Mrs. Donahue's sister, who herself was to become the reigning hostess of San Francisco, was married to Edward Martin, the founder of the Hibernia Bank. Nearly all its depositors were Irish, and it prospered by paying them interest at the extraordinary rate of 11 percent. Meanwhile, a brother to Mrs. Martin and Mrs. Donahue, John G. Downey, had come to California from County Roscommon in 1849 with $10. He had forsaken the search for gold, however, and instead opened a drugstore in Los Angeles. By the time of the Civil War, he was governor of the state.

James Phelan was born in Queens County in Ireland in 1821. He emigrated to New York as a boy, worked as a clerk in a grocery store, and then went to San Francisco to look for gold. Instead, he opened a saloon. Later he went into real estate and banking. His son, who was also James Phelan, tripled the fortune that his father left him, and then was elected Mayor. He was an honest man in what was generally accorded to be a den of thieves, and eventually he was elected to the United States Senate. Retiring from that after one term, his upright character having become a burden to other California politicians, he built a Spanish villa on a mountain sixty miles south of San Francisco, put in a swimming pool, and began to explore the delights of high life. He became a patron of the arts, bought one of the first automobiles, and served champagne at every meal. His guests always dressed for dinner.

San Francisco was always a party town, and from its beginning it had a society of sorts. Even before the Vigilantes rousted the worst of the badmen from the streets, men and women, the men outnumbering the women by approximately twenty to one, were meeting in boarding houses and hotels for polite soirées. The most fashionable boarding house of all, at the corner of Broadway and Montgomery, was built by Henry Meiggs, an Irishman who had come from New York in 1849. He had every virtue, including good looks, and he built a sawmill and wharf in North Beach, became an alderman, and then started to develop South Park, a neighborhood for the rich that was supposed to look like London's Kew Gardens.

Unfortunately, Meiggs ran out of money and began to forge first municipal notes and then the notes of private corporations. Suspicion formed about him, but one step ahead of the law he fled to Tahiti, leaving $800,000 in debts and bad notes. Eventually, he went to South America, where he became a road contractor and made millions before dying in Peru in 1877.

Besides the boarding houses, society went to the theater, and the greatest impresario in San Francisco and indeed the entire West was the Irish Catholic Tom Maguire, who had been a hackman and a saloonkeeper in New York, and then had gone to San Francisco in 1849. He was more or less unscrupulous, virtually illiterate, and generally considered one of the handsomest men in the city. He won his first wife, who was known only as Little Em, in a barroom brawl in New York when he beat up the man she was living with, and together in San Francisco they opened up the first Jenny Lind Theater. It was above a saloon and gambling house that Maguire also owned, and it went up in flames months after it was opened. Maguire built the second Jenny Lind Theater in the same place. It had 2000 seats, making it the biggest theater in the West, and also too big a place to run profitably. Maguire sold it to San Francisco for $200,000 and it became City Hall.

Next, Maguire built Maguire's Opera House. He put in a resident stock company, brought the younger Junius Brutus Booth from New York to be stage manager and began to import celebrated actors, as well as minstrels, jugglers, burlesque stars, Irish comics, and once a team of Japanese acrobats. He built other theaters, went to Europe to look for talent, and even brought back an Italian opera troupe. San Francisco, regarding Maguire as something of an attraction himself, presented him with a silver service. He was by now a distinguished figure, burly and erect, with prematurely white hair, a glorious handlebar mustache, and diamonds on his fingers and in his necktie. The great actors of the time were appearing in his theaters, and some of the great oddities, too. Oscar Wilde came, his hair parted in the middle, a sunflower in his lapel, to lecture on Irish poetry. The city's florists sold out their bunches of sunflowers in no time, and for a while, it seemed, all the gentry in San Francisco were also wearing sunflowers. Even the Irish, however, stayed away from the lectures on poetry.

In the end, Maguire's demise was as rapid as his ascent, which is also a common thing for the Irish. Little Em had never been much to look at, but she had been as shrewd in business as her husband had been daring. When she died, Maguire took as his second wife a younger woman who wore her clothes well and had lovely shoulders. He had always been a gambler, and in his distinguished clothes he had even looked like one, but now his luck was running out. When Edwin Forrest had opened at Maguire's Opera House in *Richelieu,* the demand for tickets was so great that Maguire could auction them off for as much as $500 apiece. But there were thin times coming in San Francisco, and in a few years Maguire's houses began to go dark. Maguire had been in and out of court many times over the years, forever being sued by actors to whom he had neglected to pay salaries, or playwrights to whom he had declined to pay royalties, and now the judgments were going against him. Finally, the Baldwin Theater closed. It was the theater Maguire had built with a man called Lucky Baldwin, who would himself go broke at seventy-two, then make a new fortune in the Klondike, and die worth millions at eighty-one, and it was Maguire's pride. Desperate now, he put on a passion play, but it left San Francisco appalled. The Catholics were distressed because it showed Christ and the Virgin on stage, and the Protestants were distressed because they thought the play was papist propaganda. An ordinance was passed forbidding the "impersonation of any scriptural character upon the stage of any theater."

Maguire put it on again, anyway. He had gotten away with *East Lynne* and *Camille* when they were considered risqué, and he had even showed women on stage in tights. This time, however, it was different. The police swept down and arrested Maguire's star, James O'Neill, the father of Eugene. O'Neill was freed on $100 bail, but Maguire, his time come to an end, left San Francisco and went back to New York. He died there in 1896, supported by the Actors Fund.

One way or another, in triumph or adversity, the Irish were entertaining San Francisco. South Park was the first great place for society to live, and then it was Rincon Hill, and finally, of course, there was Nob Hill. Nob Hill was lined with the mansions of the rich, and the Irish were prominent among them. In the 1870s, a writer in a San Francisco weekly described it this way: "We have a millionaire among us . . . His name is MacDooligan . . . The present partner of the joys and sorrows of MacDooligan was once the beautiful Bridget MacShinnegan . . . The MacShinnegan coat of arms is a spalpeen rampant on a field of gold . . . The family is going to Paris while father remains to superintend the erection of a palatial mansion on Nob Hill . . . Louis Quatorze? Renaissance? Their manner is now *distingué,* their society *recherché,* their manner *débonnaire,* their actions breathe a *savoir-faire.*"

The social aspirations of the Irish, or more particularly of the wives and daughters, were becoming the stuff of legends. In 1883, Mary Ellen Donahue, the daughter of the man who had given his wife a glass coach, married the Baron Henry von Schroeder in New York, having discovered him there on one of the periodic expeditions the San Francisco Irish made into Eastern society. It was among the first of many marriages between the daughters of the American rich and titled Europeans, and it was different than most of them because it survived, although not without difficulty. After their marriage, the von Schroeders returned to San Francisco and became social attractions. Eventually, Mary Ellen Donahue von Schroeder became the owner of the fashionable San Rafael Hotel. It was a social attraction, too, and in 1900 a story in the San Francisco *Morning Call* suggested that the Baron was making romantic conquests there among the summer visitors. The Baron, as befitted a man who had won the Iron Cross from Von Moltke in the Franco-Prussian War, brought suit against the *Call*. He lost.

The most celebrated of the Irish fortunes, however, were made in the gold and silver camps. Sometimes the fortunes were not as grand as they were supposed to be, but they were enough to allow wives to leave the camps and try to conquer society elsewhere and usually fail at it. There is a story about John H. Gregory, an Irish prospector who struck gold near Central City, Colorado, in 1859. "Thank God," he is supposed to have said as he threw away his pick, "now my wife can become a lady." Then there was an Irish maid called Katie. She worked for the George Tillinghast Clarks, Eastern social types who had come to Colorado to better themselves, but in time she married an Irishman who made a fortune as a flour miller. On being introduced to Mrs. Clark again, she cut her dead.

None of the Irish made important fortunes in the first gold strikes in California, but ten years later they were prominent in the discoveries in Colorado and Nevada. Gregory was one of the first, and then six months later Peter O'Riley and Patrick McLaughlin found the Comstock Lode. It was enormously rich in both gold and silver, but O'Riley and McLaughlin, with the aversion to success that the Irish show now and again, sold out for about $100,000. O'Riley built the first stone hotel in Virginia City, speculated in mining stocks, lost everything, and died in an insane asylum. McLaughlin lost his money, too, and ended up as a cook in a mining camp.

In 1873, John Mackay and James Fair made the greatest strike of all, the Bonanza. Mackay, who had been born in Dublin, went to New York as a youth and then sailed to California in 1849. He became a prospector and eventually a mining superintendent, and finally in 1868 got control of a mine. A year later he joined Fair, who had also been born in Ireland. They needed more money, however, and so they brought in James Flood and William O'Brien, two more Irishmen, and James Walker, a rich Virginian. Flood and O'Brien had run a saloon in San Francisco and then had opened the Auction Lunch Room. O'Brien, a cheerful, affable man, tended the bar in an apron and a high silk hat. Flood, a more conventional businessman, mingled with the customers and collected tips on mining stocks. He played the tips, O'Brien played along with him, and finally they made enough money to sell the Auction Lunch Room and become brokers of mining stocks themselves. The Bonanza made millionaires of all of them, and when Mackay bought out Walker's interest he became one of the richest men in the country.

The wealth changed O'Brien not at all. He said he had never sought much money, but instead had simply grabbed the tail of a kite and been "histed" up by it. His only concession to wealth seems to have been a hideous mausoleum he built for himself in Calvary Cemetery in San Francisco, where he was buried five years after the Bonanza strike. Flood also stayed on in San Francisco, where he put up a great chocolate-colored mansion on Nob Hill. Fair became a United States senator, treated his wife badly, and alienated nearly everyone with a gaudy display of wealth and monumental rudeness. Fair's son drank himself to death at an early age, although his daughters did better. One of them, Tessie, married the wealthy Hermann Oelrichs; the other, Birdie, married the even wealthier William K. Vanderbilt. Together they became queens in the Gilded Age of Newport.

Mackay, the richest of the old partners, stayed on in Virginia City at first managing the Bonanza, but eventually investing his money in telegraph lines and a transatlantic cable company. As his wealth grew, so did his wife's social designs. She was the daughter of a barber and sometime soldier called Hungerford, and she had met Mackay after her first husband died. Destitute, she had been alone in Nevada with an infant daughter, and some miners had sought to take up a collection for her. Mackay married her instead. It was a good marriage, but Mrs. Mackay hated Virginia City and wanted glory in larger spheres. New York had been the city of her childhood, and there, she thought, as the wife of the famous mining millionaire, she would triumph. She did not. Stories about her having been an Irish washerwoman reached New York before she did, and she was badly snubbed. She fled to Paris, hired a diplomat's wife to tell her what the social game was all about, and then moved to London, where she took a house near Buckingham Palace. Soon she was receiving the Prince of Wales, Ulysses S. Grant, and nearly anyone else she chose to. Her daughter by her first marriage became the Italian Princess of Colonna, although the Prince turned out to be a rotter. Mrs. Mackay never really tried to conquer New York again, but her son, Clarence Hungerford Mackay, whose daughter Ellin married Irving Berlin, did it easily.

Margaret Tobin Brown also tried to conquer society, but she never came even remotely close, and instead she left behind a series of stories about herself, most of which were untrue. For one thing, she has passed into history as the wife of "Leadville Johnny" Brown, when actually she was married to one James J. Brown. Leadville Johnny was his employer, the owner of the richest mine in Leadville, Colorado, and he had given Brown only a share in the mine. It was big enough, however, to allow his wife to open up a mansion in Denver and to try to get on with the members of society, who simply declined to recognize her. She was once a housemaid, and for that matter she still rather looked like one. She gave parties to which no one came, sent stories and pictures to society editors that were never used, and in general made a pest of herself. Rejected, she went to Europe, where she said she had far more money than she did, and took to carrying a tall crooked duchess's cane, just like Madame Du Barry.

Her husband, an amiable Irishman who preferred a night out with the boys to any of this, disappeared for a while, and that was why she was alone when she boarded the *Titanic* on its maiden voyage. Five nights later, the *Titanic* hit an iceberg, and Mrs. Brown found herself in lifeboat No. 6 with twenty-eight other people. She swore at them. She cajoled them. She told jokes. She even brandished the Colt .45 she carried in her fur muff, and somehow she kept them rowing the lifeboat. When they were picked up and reporters asked her about it, she dismissed her performance as unimportant. "I had typical Brown luck," she said. "I'm unsinkable."

So, Margaret Tobin Brown became immortalized as "the unsinkable Molly Brown." She now had all the publicity she had ever dreamed of, but sadly it wasn't enough. She said that she had far more money than ever before, spread stories about her impending elevation into the British peerage, and moved in increasingly eccentric ways through the great hotels of London, Paris, and Nice. James Brown died broke in 1922. She died ten years later, living in a single room in a hotel in New York, still carrying her duchess's cane.

V

Southampton: Days of Grace

THE PRECISE MOMENT when the Irish Catholics passed truly into society is unclear, but it is almost certain that the place where it happened was Southampton. True, there were Irish living in the marbled sepulchers of Newport, but Newport was full of the gaudy rich, meat packers, steel barons, and oil men, who looked for something they could not find in Cleveland, say, or Detroit, and who went to Newport to be snubbed and to indulge themselves in the innocent vulgarity that only the seriously rich can afford. The members of the 400 had gone to Newport first, causing a colony of artists and writers to flee in some horror, and while there were Catholics among the 400, there were no identifiable Irish Catholics, the first Irish Catholic of great prominence in Newport being Mrs. Hermann Oelrichs, the daughter of James Fair of the Comstock fortune. Theresa, or Tessie, Oelrichs followed an honorable tradition among the great ladies of Newport: she went mad. Mrs. William Backhouse Astor, *the* Mrs. Astor, who for years presided over Newport in diamond stomachers and solitary majesty, died in 1908, and in her last summers there she stood alone in the drawing room of her mansion, exchanging pleasantries with people who had long since passed on. Tessie Fair Oelrichs, a pleasant old soul, who shunned a maid and would scrub the floors of her mansion, Rosecliff, herself, tried but never could inherit Mrs. Astor's title as queen of Newport, although she did manage to be like her at the very end. Tessie, a wraith of what she had once been, would wander the halls of Rosecliff, also being hospitable to people who weren't there. Things like this always seemed to be happening in Newport. Its splendor was contrived, attended by enormous publicity, and therefore seriously deleterious to the Irish. Their progress, as the financial writers once said about the financier Thomas Fortune Ryan, had to be "noiseless." When it was not, the Irish, who were always self-conscious about themselves, would fall on their faces in deplorable ways, or what was worse, often cease to be Catholics.

Southampton was right for them. Southampton, said one of its great ladies, Mrs. Goodhue Livingston, was a "backwater of God," which is an imprecise-enough description, but at least suggestive of the kind of thing that was good about the place. It was nothing more than a sleepy, pleasant village in 1875, when a dry goods merchant from New York built a cottage there and then a few years later persuaded his doctor to build a cottage there, too. This was the beginning of Southampton as a summer resort, and it more or less officially became a place for the fashionable rich when a family from New York, back from a trip to Venice, brought a gondola with them and floated it on Lake Agawam. Soon, the Irish Catholics began coming, with the first of stature being Judge Morgan O'Brien, who carried himself and his daughters over from Hampton Bays and put up a house that looked like a yellow pagoda on the shore of Lake Agawam. Finley Peter Dunne, the creator of "Mr. Dooley," came to Southampton, and so did a political type called Patrick Francis Murphy, and together they all joined the Southampton Club, whose president was the starchy Nicholas Murray Butler, who was president of Columbia University as well. The interesting thing about this, aside from the fact that the Irish were there at all, was that O'Brien, Dunne, and Murphy were also members of the Occasional Thinkers, a kind of club within the Southampton Club, over which Dr. Butler also presided. Butler, his friends said, found the Irishmen attractive, and the Irishmen, using him and the Southampton Club as the impeccable references they were, soon found their way into the imposing Union Club in New York.

So, Southampton, if not eager to have the Irish upon it, had seen some of the breed and would probably be at least civil when more came, and when the inventor Thomas E. Murray bought a summer home there in 1927 it meant that the Irish were coming in abundance. Murray bought a great shingled house on the ocean called Wickapogue, and then his daughter Anna and her husband, James McDonnell, bought a house virtually next door. Meanwhile, Thomas E. Murray, Jr., and his wife, who back in Brooklyn had been spending every night of their lives going across the street to visit the older Murrays, certainly would not desert them now and so they bought a house on Gin Lane in Southampton. Immediately, the Joseph B. Murrays moved to Water Mill, which is just next to South-ampton, and then Julia and Lester Cuddihy went there, and soon Catherine McQuail, by now separated from her husband, went to Southampton, and then the moody Jack Murray and his family came, too. It was the way of great Irish families in those days to cling together for protection, and it meant that in the space of a season or two the whole family, with the exception of Marie, the daughter who had married a Protes-tant and wisely chose to stay on in Connecticut, had de-scended on Southampton all in a bunch. Now, the family did not know it, and Southampton may only have suspected it, but in time the family would rather transform it. In the late 1920s, Southampton was a quiet place, known mostly for a golf course that had opened in 1891 with little Shinnecock Indian boys as caddies, the Irving Hotel and its rocking chairs, and a social life that was run by some elderly ladies of elegant

breeding who collectively were known as "the dreadnaughts."
Southampton had never had many of the flashy rich, and even
the names of its streets — Job's Lane, Meeting House Lane,
First Neck Lane — discouraged the merely frivolous, even had
they been able to afford a house there. Any resort has syba-
rites, but Southampton when the Murrays and McDonnells
went there had fewer than most, and the proper Episcopalians
who attended St. Andrew's Dune Church were a great deal
like the Irish Catholic Murrays and McDonnells, who straight-
away began going to the Church of the Sacred Hearts of Jesus
and Mary. Neither group knew it about the other, but at
bottom they were all Puritans, and in any contest between
Puritans the ones who believe they are closest to God will
always win. This meant the Episcopalians hadn't a chance.

Still, it is hard to know now what Southampton thought
about those people who fell upon it in those early summers.
The Murrays and McDonnells never really knew themselves,
although being Irish they had their suspicions, which, naturally, were unpleasant ones. "I'm sure everyone thought they
were being inundated by the Mickey Irish," says the daughter
of Jack Murray who later married Alfred Gwynne Vanderbilt.
"I could sense their antagonism even as a child," says her
sister, the Marquesa di Montezemolo, who for years was fashion editor of *Vogue*. "Mother always thought the WASPs
resented us as upstarts, and when I grew older and met the
parents of some of my friends I thought so, too. We were
never invited to the parties that the really social people had.
They thought we were nouveau." One of her cousins, a
daughter of Julia and Lester Cuddihy, remembers being in the
family bathhouse at the Southampton Beach Club and over-
hearing one of the very social Schumacher girls in the next
bathhouse. "Southampton," she said, "is being positively
swamped by all those Irish." The Cuddihy girl says that the
Schumacher girl sounded disturbed. Mrs. Marie Harris, a
daughter of Thomas E. Murray, Jr., says she is sure that the

general feeling in Southampton was one of disdain, but that even this was tempered. "The really aristocratic ones like Washie [Washington] Irving and his sister Kitty didn't talk badly about the Irish at all," she says. "They were always nice to us, and if anything we had chips on our shoulders because of their Harvard accents." Now this, of course, is getting close to the heart of things. The Irish Catholics carried their sensibilities closer to the surface than most people did, and forever expecting a rebuff they built up their own resentments. Moreover, they could be eminent snobs themselves.

The McDonnells were the richest branch of the family and generally considered the most social, although in an Irish Catholic world that certainly never meant very much. "In the beginning," says one of the McDonnell girls, Mrs. Charlotte Harris, who married into a Catholic family that owned a steamship line, "we used to sit by ourselves outside the beach club, all alone, all in a row. People called us the Irish group. Later they called us the Spellman group. I don't know why we sat alone. We were afraid, or shy, or something. Then we sat by ourselves because we wanted to. By God, we were going to show *them*." Now *them* in this case meant Southampton at large, but as the years at Southampton went by, the Murrays and McDonnells decided that they were showing the other Irish Catholics, too. Everyone in the family knew the Kennedys, for example, and when they moved from Boston to New York in the 1930s, Rose Kennedy and Anna McDonnell, recognizing each other as being cut from the same stuff, became particularly close. The feeling among the Murrays and McDonnells, though, was that the Kennedys weren't quite right, that they were, well, nouveau, and when Mrs. Kennedy visited Mrs. McDonnell at Southampton the family simply assumed that she was there to find out how she, too, could set a table, or arrange the flowers, or whatever it was one was supposed to do.

"She and her daughters were being snubbed terribly in New

York," a Murray lady recalls, "so she'd come to Auntie Anna for advice. She would be driven up in a big black car, and we'd all say, 'Doesn't she know that out here she should be driving a station wagon?' My mother was at the McDonnells one day that Mrs. Kennedy was there, and she came back and said, 'Rose Kennedy, such a lovely person, but what a dreadful voice she has.' Mother couldn't get over it. Then, when Joe Kennedy was appointed Ambassador to England there were all those pictures of the Kennedys in the papers. We all thought, 'How dowdy, how unchic, how *Irish Catholic!*' We should have been going to England, not them." But the Kennedys did go to England, and when they got there they found that the ladies from New York who wanted to have their daughters presented at Court had to make their appeals through Ambassador Kennedy. The story is that Mrs. Kennedy got the list of supplicants, took a pencil, and with great satisfaction, one by one, crossed out the names of the women who had once been rude to her. The Murray and McDonnell ladies said they knew exactly how she felt.

There was never much flamboyance about these Irish, but because they were Irish, and in the case of the Murrays and McDonnells because there were so many of them, people insisted in seeing something like a raffishness about them. In fact, sometimes the Murrays and McDonnells invited it on themselves. On the first Fourth of July that Thomas E. Murray was at Wickapogue, he assembled his relatives about him and announced that in the evening he would put on a display of fireworks. It would be at the home of Thomas E. Murray, Jr., on Gin Lane, he said, and it would be a proper family entertainment, attended by parents, children, the help, and even the pets. Accordingly, a groom that evening began laying everything out on top of a sand dune for what was to be that most American of entertainments. He put out Roman candles, St. Catherine's wheels, Greek fire, everything, and when the family was gathered and Thomas E. Murray gave the signal he proudly touched off the first Roman candle. Off in a shower of sparks it went, only not out to sea, but sideways into the next Roman candle, which went into the rest of the Roman candles, which touched off the St. Catherine's wheels, which ignited the Greek fire, which set off everything else. It was a marvelous sight, and it was made all the more marvelous by the fire it started in the dune grass. Up and down the dunes the fire spread, lighting the skies, and bringing one of the Murray's Irish maids to her window in a small fit of ecstasy. "O, what a beautiful display," she said, while below her a small Murray child cried out in fear. "Shut up," Thomas E. Murray bellowed, and a small McDonnell child, caught up in the wonder of it all, said, "Ooo, Grandpa said, 'Shut up.' " The flames by now were threatening the homes on either side of them. The children were dancing round and about, and Grandpa was bellowing louder than ever. To this day, one of his grandsons says, it was quite the most exciting thing he has ever seen. Someone called the Southampton Fire Department, and when it came with all its equipage and volunteers the townspeople met the Murrays, McDonnells, and Cuddihys for the first time. The volunteers, spraying chemicals all about, put out the fire and left in its place a couple of acres of blackened and sere dunes. All that summer and the next people drove up Gin Lane to see them and to wonder what kind of people would do such a thing, while the families in the houses on either side of the blackened dunes would regard the Murrays and McDonnells with suspicion for years. A boy from one of the families, feeling that he had a special grievance, once held the head of a Murray girl underwater so long that she was quite certain he intended to drown her. The members of the other family were considerably more circumspect. They were forever after condescending to the Murrays and McDonnells, which, of course, was hitting them right where they lived, and sometimes they cut them dead altogether. The head of that family, who was the chairman of the board of the National City Bank, was later indicted for income tax evasion. It gave the Murrays and McDonnells a quiet satisfaction.

In an odd way, the most flamboyant thing the Murrays and McDonnells ever did in Southampton was to withdraw from it and to set up something like a community of their own. It was not intended to be this, but it became an Irish Catholic retreat, and eventually a place of fascination to the gossip columnists, who, like the people in Southampton, were always confused about which Murrays and McDonnells were living there. Actually, it was only three families living on a great plot of land by the ocean, but the families grew so large that there always seemed to be more of them than there really were, and to this day Southampton can scarcely separate the strains of Irish that sprang from the retreat. It began with the death of Thomas E. Murray in 1929, when his son Thomas E. Murray ascended into Wickapogue, and then bought more acres of his own. Anna and James McDonnell were living next to him, separated by only two swimming pools in between. Subsequently, Julia and Lester Cuddihy, although they lived in Water Mill, bought a strip of land near both of them as a speculation. Then, Jack Murray, who had sold out just before the Crash, paid $125,000 and got an adjacent fifty-six acres and the houses on them for his property. It meant that the McDonnells, the Tom Murrays and the Jack Murrays, and all their establishments were now dwelling together just outside the village of Southampton on some 160 acres, which included their own small lake. It was inevitable that they would not dwell together in perfect harmony, but in the beginning who could tell that?

Jack Murray's place was called Lighthouse Farm and it had behind it a stable, a garage, laundry, chicken coop, caretaker's house, and cottage for the groom. There was a field for growing vegetables, too. Tom Murray's house was bigger than Jack's and it had even more buildings scattered around it. The McDonnells had only their cottage, without other buildings, but in the cottage were ten bedrooms, a music room, library, living room, dining room, breakfast room, poolroom and two kitchens, all of which, except the kitchens, were done up graciously in chintz and deep rugs by the McMillen decorators in New York. The McDonnell cottage also had rooms for the help, but apparently no one ever thought to count them. Driven by some insatiable lust, perhaps their only one, the McDonnells and Tom Murrays kept adding terraces, rooms, and whole wings to their houses, and whenever they did a priest would come in and bless each one. The priest would pray, make the sign of the Cross, and then sprinkle holy water. The family, meanwhile, would be following the priest about, and soon he would turn and bless them, too. The terrace, or the room, or the wing would now be open.

The Jack Murrays had seven children, the Tom Murrays had eleven, and the McDonnells had fourteen. "I'm afraid to dive in," Al Smith, a frequent visitor to the pool, would say. "I might swallow a baby." Outside the compound, in Southampton, the Joseph Murrays had five children, while in Water Mill the Cuddihys had seven children and Catherine McQuail had two. There was a confusion of children, furthering the suspicion that the Irish by propagation alone were taking over Southampton, and leading Newell Tilton, a society man from there, Palm Beach, Tuxedo, and Newport, to suggest that perhaps the place should now be called "Murray Bay." The dutiful Anna McDonnell had people to help her with her fourteen children, but being dutiful she insisted on accompanying each of them on every visit they made to a doctor, a dentist, or even to a clothing store. Once, she took nine of them to Hildreth's in Southampton to buy shoes. One by one they filed in and were fitted, and when Mrs. McDonnell was presented with the bill she examined it in her careful way and then protested to the clerk that it wasn't enough. "Oh, madam," he said, "we always give reductions to institutions."

In truth, the McDonnell cottage was run something like an institution, and by the time of Southampton Mrs. McDonnell was becoming something of an institution herself. For one thing, she was elegant, the elegance being neither Irish, nor Catholic, nor for that matter even particularly American; it was a very quiet elegance, which meant it was more nearly French. "If I could only look like Anna McDonnell after having had all those children," Rose Kennedy said, and when the family heard that it understood perfectly. Anna McDonnell was special; so was her sister-in-law Marie Murray, but Anna McDonnell was supposed to be perfection. She had given birth to all those children and always she had declined anesthetics, saying instead that she would offer up the pain to the glory of God. "To offer it up," to find sanctity in suffering, to find comfort and even joy in it, was the most Irish Catholic of impulses, conditioned by a thousand years of the race, by the clergy, and by all that had happened to both. Anna McDonnell would not wilt in the heat of any Southampton summer; she would always be there, perfectly controlled, outwardly assured, impervious, it seemed, to either frivolity or discomfort. There was the little dress, the little hat, the little veil, all coming from the little shop on East 60th Street that was run by an Irish Catholic lady and greatly favored by other Irish Catholic ladies, and always there were the shoes with the pointed toes, the strap over the instep and the Louis XVI heels, and above the appearance of elegance there was the appearance of propriety. There was nothing so important to that generation as propriety, and in this the Irish part and the Catholic part strengthened each other nicely and became so inseparable that you could not imagine one without the other. A slip, a failure, the smallest lapse from the prescribed faith, and these Irish would fear they were no longer Catholics, that their souls were lost. A slip, a failure, the smallest lapse from the prescribed behavior, and these Irish would fear they were no longer acceptable, that their positions were lost. There was a great deal of fear involved in all this, but who on the outside would ever know that?

Therefore, Anna McDonnell, the only one of her generation who had talked back to her father, was not about to be caught up now in seasonal social conventions. The demands of church and of blood were too great, and at Southampton she ran a staff of thirteen — butler, chauffeur, two nurses, two cooks, two kitchen maids, four chambermaids, and a gardener — as rigorously as she ran herself. Every morning she got up, went to Mass, had breakfast, and then at nine drove her station wagon to Bohack's to do the day's marketing. She planned each meal, pondered each leftover, and in her unruffled way saw to it that things were exactly as they ought to be. This may not sound like any particular accomplishment, but among rich ladies of her generation, who were paying their Irish help $50 a month to do these things for them, it was practically unheard of, not so eccentric as Tessie Fair Oelrichs scrubbing her own floor, but quite enough to lift Anna McDonnell above the other rich ladies who lived in splendid establishments in Southampton. The boys at Bohack's, aware that they were in something of a presence, would load up the station wagon, and Anna McDonnell, wrapped splendidly in the faith and the knowledge that the Kingdom of Heaven is won only a step at a time, would drive herself back to the cottage.

Then, with the utmost regularity every afternoon, Anna McDonnell and Marie Murray would retreat to the private chapel of Thomas E. Murray, Jr. Archbishop Molloy had seen to it that he had the privilege of the chapel, the same as his father before him, and it was a small and beautiful thing, with dark panels, a wooden altar, and a plain gold cross. There were the Stations of the Cross on the wall, and prie-dieux covered with velvet for the ladies to kneel on. While their peers at Southampton had tea, or sat about at the Beach Club, Anna McDonnell and Marie Murray would stay in the chapel for a holy hour, sixty minutes of prayers, readings, or other devotions, communing with their God and fortifying themselves against whatever it was that lay outside the gates of the compound. It had no hedges in those days, and it stretched from the ocean back over the dunes, past the houses and across the fields to the blacktop road that went into the village of Southampton. Among other things, the village had Peck & Peck, Foulke & Foulke, Charles of the Ritz, and Bendel's, but the place where the Murrays and McDonnells went most often was the Church of the Sacred Hearts on Hill Street. Its pastor was Father George Killeen, and he was a beefy, reddened man, with a large shock of hair and a boom-ing brogue that was partly Irish, but mostly all his own. The "blesd virge" he would say, and mean the "blessed Virgin," and frequently he would preach about "storming the gates of Heaven," which would befuddle the youngest Murrays and McDonnells. Father Killeen was never accused of flouting the legalisms of church doctrine in favor of their spirit, and con-firmed in his own sanctity he often judged that of others. The Tom Murray, Jrs., and the McDonnells seemed to like that about him, probably because he confirmed the contours of their own existence so well, although some of the children, trooping to confession in squads every Saturday, became dis-comfited by his habit of shouting at them from the confes-sional booth. "Bless me, Father, for I have sinned," the children would begin, and it hardly seemed to matter whether the sin was mortal or venial. Father Killeen would give them hell just the same.

Of all the priests who were in and out of the family com-

Thomas E. Murray and his family in 1905. *Clockwise, from left to right:*
Thomas E. Jr. (wearing glasses), Joseph, Mrs. Thomas E. Murray with
Marie in her arms, Daniel, Anna, Thomas E. Murray, John, Catherine,
and Julia.

The patriarch: Thomas E. Murray.
Born 1860. Died 1929.

Outside Thomas E. Murray's house on St. Mark's Avenue, Brooklyn, in 1906. Anna is third from the left in the bottom row, next to her brother John in the car; their sister Julia is second from the right. Their young friends are all Irish.

Mrs. Thomas E. Murray
and three of her daughters
around 1915. *Left to right:*
Catherine, Mrs. Murray,
Anna, and Julia.

Members of the third generation with their grandmother, Mrs. Thomas
E. Murray, at her home in Brooklyn, about 1925. *Top row, left to right:*
Lester Cuddihy, Rosamund Murray, James Murray, Mrs. Murray, Mary
Jane Cuddihy, Patricia Murray. *Bottom row:* Jeanne Murray, Theresa
Murray, Catherine McDonnell, Thomas E. Murray III, Marie Murray.

John F. Murray, who was called Jack, and his son John Jr. in Southampton about 1930.

Anna and James McDonnell outside the Southampton Riding and Hunting Club in 1940.

Anna and James McDonnell and their 14 children in their Fifth Avenue apartment in 1936. Seated in the front row, left to right: Mary, Barbara, Morgan, and Marjorie. Behind them are Murray, Sheila, James Jr., Mrs. McDonnell, holding Sean, Genevieve, Gerald, and Charlotte. Standing are Anne, Mr. McDonnell, Catherine, and Charles.

The beach outside the Southampton Bathing Corporation (or, as it is usually called, the Beach Club) in 1936. Some of the men still cling to wing collars.

Right: Cardinal Pacelli on his visit to America in 1936, with William Cardinal O'Connell of Boston to his right and Francis J. Spellman to his left. Spellman was then a bishop in Boston.

Coaching at the Southampton Riding and Hunting Club in the 1930s. The girls, from left to right, are Jeanne Murray, a friend, Marcia Murray, Catherine McDonnell, Rosamund Murray, and Marie Murray.

Henry Ford dancing with
his grandson's new bride,
the former Anne McDonnell,
at her Southampton wedding
in 1940.

The former Jeanne Murray
and Alfred Gwynne Vanderbilt
just after their marriage
in 1945.

Top: The dining room at the Grosse Pointe Country Club on the night of Charlotte Ford's coming-out party in 1959. The room is decorated with crystal trees. *Bottom:* The receiving line. Charlotte Ford is at the left, next to her mother, while her father, Henry Ford II, kisses a guest's hand.

Charlotte Ford and Stavros Niarchos in St. Moritz after their marriage in December, 1965. He was 56; she was 24.

T. Murray McDonnell and his frequent guest, Jacqueline Onassis, hunting in Peapack, New Jersey, in 1968.

Francis Cardinal Spellman
and Bishop Fulton Sheen in
the late 1960s.

Anne McDonnell
Ford and her mother,
Anna McDonnell,
after Mass at
St. Vincent Ferrer in
New York, 1967.

The McDonnells in the late 1960s. *Standing, from left to right:* Sean, Murray, Anne, Catherine, Charlotte, Barbara, Charles, Mary, and Gerald. *Seated:* Morgan, Sheila, James, Mrs. McDonnell, Genevieve, and Marjorie.

pound in those summers, Father Killeen was the most ubiqui-
tous. He was always there, it seemed, stuffed into a scratchy
black woolen bathing suit, flopping in and out of the swimming pool, and looking, some of the children thought, rather
like a piece of wurst. In the afternoons he played golf with
Catherine McQuail. Mrs. McQuail, separated, though of
course not divorced from her husband, Ennis, needed a golf
partner, and in the way of the Irish Catholic she was she had
chosen the priest. The meaner spirits in Southampton said
there were unspeakable things going on between those two,
but the meaner spirits could only speculate, and they never
understood it. There is a sexual relationship between the
priests and their ladies, but it is a surrogate one, and therefore
not to be confused with the real thing.

Father Killeen was part of that tradition, and he was part of
another one, too, of the Irish American priest who is both
sword of the Lord and retainer to the rich. It is a difficult
thing for a man to be, leaving room for a subtle corruption of
the souls of both the priest and the rich, and sometimes in the
recesses of his spirit the priest knows it. Then he may become
more full of bonhomie than ever before, showing that it
doesn't bother him, or else he may become more judgmental
and querulous, and ease his spirit by mortifying his own and
everyone else's flesh, too. Father Killeen chose to do both,
sputtering and splashing about in the pool in rough good
humor, and whenever he could reminding everyone that damnation was just around the corner for even the smallest infrac-
tion. The family, being Irish, put up with it. Father Killeen
sniffed and complained, and said that so many Murrays and
McDonnells were attending Mass in the private chapel on
Sundays that the collections at the Church of the Sacred
Hearts were suffering. Henceforth, the family took up a collection in their chapel on Sundays and turned it over to him.
Later on, he spoke hopefully of becoming a monsignor, and

so Thomas E. Murray, Jr., by now risen high in the councils of the laity, saw to it that this too came to pass. Father Killeen had a proprietary interest in the family, and most of the family had a proprietary interest in him. Nonetheless, some members of the family were skeptical, but being of the generation they were, and believing that a priest was still a priest, they would hardly do much about it. On Sundays, Father Killeen would stand on the steps of his church, a railroad watch in hand, and count the Murrays and McDonnells as they came in, family by family, until only the Jack Murrays were left. They would always be the last to arrive, and Father Killeen, looking soberly at his watch, and then reproachfully at Jack Murray, would say, "Ah, Jack, out late again last night?" and Jack, looking straight at Father Killeen, would say, "Yes, Father, and drunk as a lord." It was a small gesture, but it was all Jack's own, and followed by his wife and seven children he would walk down the aisle of the church, where row on row of other Murrays and McDonnells, quiet, composed, and hardly rustling, would be clutching their missals, just possibly bored and longing to be elsewhere, but no doubt offering it up just the same.

Jack Murray spent five years of the 1930s in his dying, and in the end he had been in such pain that even the touch of the sheets on his body was more than he could bear. Cirrhosis of the liver, the doctor said, but there was the melancholia, too, and when the doctor suggested again that Jack should see a psychiatrist Jack would have none of it. He went through those last years in pain of one kind or another, grew further apart from his brothers and sisters, and just before his death wanted to bring suit against them over what was left of their father's estate. Jack and Jeanne Murray had always been outside the family, and as the years went on their children began to feel that they were outside it, too. James McDonnell always made it clear that his children would never attend any-

thing but Catholic schools, and so Jack would beckon one of
his own sons from time to time and say, "Run over and tell
your Uncle James that you're going to Yale and you're going
to hell." It wasn't much of a joke, but Jack really didn't know
anything else to do. Things hadn't worked out for him quite
the way he had hoped, although he was such a careless mix-
ture of charm and insouciance that it was hard to guess even
about that. He had a siren on his car, and when he went to
Southampton he would get off the train at Hampton Bays,
jump into the car, and then, siren wailing gloriously, race the
train all the way home. His brothers and sisters hardly approved of it. At twenty-nine, Jack had run for governor of the
New York Stock Exchange and had taken his friend Al Smith
onto the balcony of the Exchange with him, hoping to sway
the votes of the men on the floor below, but that, of course,
hadn't worked at all with those Protestant Republican stockbrokers.

When Jack was a commissioner of the Port of New York,
he had conceived an ambitious plan to extend the Holland
Tunnel across Manhattan and into Brooklyn, but he had been
voted down on that and taken to brooding about it. In 1934,
he managed Herbert H. Lehman's campaign for Governor of
New York, and when Lehman won Jack had hoped for a
major appointment, but that hadn't come, either, and so Jack
had speculated to Jeanne about going into real estate, or public relations, or any of a dozen other things. He did none of
them, and one Sunday morning at Southampton he began to
hemorrhage. He was taken back to Brooklyn in an ambulance, and the ambulance was accompanied by a state trooper
who used the siren on his car nearly all the way back to the
city. Had Jack been conscious he would have loved it. He
died later at his home in Brooklyn, still a skeptic, but also a
Murray, and so his solemn High Requiem Mass was celebrated by three bishops, seven monsignors, and thirty priests,

and he was buried on the day before his thirty-eighth birthday.

It must not be thought in all this, however, that the family was a joyless mélange, measuring its days in communion wafers and plenary indulgences, or going through life without the simple pleasures of the rich. Almost from the beginning at Southampton, the Murrays and McDonnells were doing things that had nothing to do with being either Irish or Catholic, and were attractive enough to set the society columnists to writing about them. The first and most tireless chronicler was the late Maury Paul, a plump, perfumed little man, who was William Randolph Hearst's first Cholly Knickerbocker. With one thing or another, Hearst was an irregular Catholic, but the society pages of the *New York Times* and the *Herald Tribune* seldom recognized any Catholics, and Irish Catholics not at all. Consequently, Hearst's editors, reacting to this and to osmotic pressure from their boss, began to specialize in them. Maury Paul, who, Cleveland Amory tells us, invented the term "café society" one day in 1919 when he noticed that the Old Guard of society apparently had disappeared the night before, was always looking for new faces and in the 1930s he discovered the Murrays and McDonnells. Their names began to turn up with increasing frequency in his columns about Southampton, and sometimes he seemed to think they had invented the place. It was a turning point in the family's history, not so dramatic perhaps as Thomas E. Murray's building his first steam engine, but seductive enough to some of his grandchildren so that in time they would court publicity and society so fiercely that it would undo them.

Nonetheless, in the beginning it was all more innocent than that, and the columnists wrote about the family mostly because the children were numerous, good-looking, and full of what was supposed to be a Celtic joie de vivre. In fact, they were the golden Irish, removed by birth and circumstance from their tribal past, although not so far removed that they were without at least a few of its warm consolations. Ahead, for some of them, were divorces, abortions, psychiatrists, and bankruptcies, but growing up in the decade of the thirties they were the most favored children of all, and they had, it seemed, everything.

There were the dances on soft summer nights at the Meadow Club, the Riding Club, the Shinnecock Golf Club. The girls wore cotton dresses and the boys wore blue blazers, and everyone who saw them knew they were a part of that big, golden family, even if they couldn't be sure which part they were. There were the sailing races off Westhampton, where one child or another would always win something, and there were the swimming and diving contests at the Beach Club, where they always won something else. Their days were full of grace, and when they played tennis at the Meadow Club, or golf at Shinnecock, the Irish chauffeurs who waited outside, all laced up into their stiff tunics of black, or clay, or fawn, would look on them and know they were Irish children, but quite unlike any they had ever seen before. These children were always riding horses, and going out with the Southampton Hunt Club, and competing all over Long Island in horse shows, and winning quantities of ribbons and trophies. The horse in America is nearly always an impulse of the second-generation rich, and so even Thomas E. Murray, Jr., skittering about his front lawn, had discovered the joys of polo, while his brothers and sisters, not caring about being atop horses themselves, saw to it that their children could ride and jump whenever they wanted to. The children could do most things that they wanted to, and when the wife of Thomas E. Murray, Jr., told her husband that Marie, their oldest daughter, wanted to have a coming-out party, he had said it was ridiculous, that he had never heard of such a thing, and that coming-out parties were for people quite unlike themselves. Then, of course, he softened, warmed toward it, in fact, and decided that Marie would have a party after all.

"I guess if she wants it she can have it" was all that he said to his wife, but then Thomas E. Murray, Jr., went ahead and had a huge platform built atop the dunes, and around it he put up a tent. The party was on the Labor Day weekend in 1939, and the flowers had died weeks before, and so Tom Murray had gladioli planted everywhere. Louis Sherry was called in to do the catering, and Eleanor Holm was hired from Billy Rose's Aquacade to swim in the pool for entertainment. The man who parked the cars had M-U-R-R-A-Y on his cap in gold braid. Some 800 people were invited, and the only small shadow on Marie Murray's life was her cousin Anne McDonnell. Anne had just announced her engagement to Henry Ford and was getting so much publicity in the papers that Marie's party was being ignored. Still, Marie had a very good party. Her father called up a team of men from New York, and that night they put on a display of fireworks. It was spectacular, with blazing horses chasing blazing men over the skies of Southampton, and for the dénouement a picture of Marie, unmistakably Marie, etched in the sand with more fireworks. The party went on all night and at dawn the younger guests, in an explosion of innocence, but feeling full of both devilment and romance, went to the 5:00 A.M. Mass at the Church of the Sacred Hearts. Father Killeen, seizing the moment for all it was worth, preached at length to these drowsy and slightly drunken young people on the value of a Catholic education, and when he was done they went back to the tent on the dunes, where Louis Sherry cooked scrambled eggs and bacon for them, and where they sat about and mooned over one another and what was really the ending of a way of life for all of them.

VI

Cardinals, Priests, and Acolytes

BEING A CATHOLIC has never offered much in the way of social prestige in America, and being an Irish Catholic traditionally has offered even less. Baltimore, New Orleans, and St. Louis society have a history of being warm to Catholics, Baltimore because of the Carrolls and all they stood for, and New Orleans and St. Louis because they had an old Creole aristocracy, but by and large it has been better in the rest of America to have been an Episcopalian. There are similarities in the appurtenances of Episcopalianism and Catholicism, with the liturgy and lovely manners of the one often like those of the other, although the Episcopal Church never had to put up with the Irish, and that made all the difference in the world. The Irish became the leading constituents of the Catholic Church in America, and from the very beginning it was obvious that they would run it, too. The first Bishop to the New World came to Haiti in 1493 and had his church consecrated on the Feast of the Epiphany the next year. He was a subject of Spain, and not much is known about him except that his name was Bernard Boyl and that he was Irish. This was how it started, with an Irish bishop ministering to a Spanish flock, and in time the Irish would spread through the hierarchy and make it their own.

In the last century, Irish prelates like Cardinal Gibbons, Archbishop Ireland, and Bishop Spalding were the church's great idea men, but time passes and in this century the Irish prelates would be known less for their thinking than for their style. One of the great seigniors, for example, was William Cardinal O'Connell of Boston, who, on hearing that his Auxilliary Bishop had just been appointed Archbishop of New York, sniffed and said, "Francis epitomizes what happens to a bookkeeper when you teach him to read." He was talking about Francis Spellman, who would become a cardinal himself, but would never achieve O'Connell's high Roman flourish. O'Connell, who died in 1944, was a man of cultivation and intelligence, and also deeply attached to the ways of the rich. He lived with a certain elegance himself, residing in a mansion in Boston, spending the winters on his estate in Nassau, and going abroad so often that he was called "Gangplank Bill." He made friends among the Boston Brahmins, just as early in his life when he was rector of the American College in Rome he had made friends among the fashionable rich who surrounded the Vatican court. "I went not frequently, but at least occasionally, to those great houses and kept in touch, and obtained a very considerable knowledge of how the world was run in general from those who, by their power and influence, were really running it," the Cardinal said in his autobiography. Then he went on to say, "And as I look back through all the changes that have happened since, I am more and more thoroughly convinced that the pontificate of Leo XIII created in Rome the very finest type that the social world had seen or will see for many a long day."

Even for a cardinal, however, much less a parish priest, it is often difficult to mix in the social world, and sometimes there is a loss of dignity. If he is able to, a priest can make it easier by believing that he has been ordained to be like the rich, and that their ways are his ways, or else he can find a power over the rich in being incorruptible. Cardinal O'Connell did mostly the first, but his successor, Richard Cardinal Cushing, practiced the second and made incorruptibility into almost an art form. Cushing, who said he wanted to spend his declining years away from all worldly luxury and out somewhere in a mission post, was the man who could not be bought, and from this strength came his benevolence, omniscience, and protection for the rich, and sometimes a little servility, too. Like Cardinal O'Connell, Cushing was a boy from a lower-middle-class family of many children, which is the background of most celebrated Irish priests, and in a speech at a labor convention he seemed pleased about it. "In all the American hierarchy resident in the United States," he said, "there is not known to me one bishop, archbishop, or cardinal whose father or mother was a college graduate. Every one of our bishops and archbishops is the son of a working man and a working man's wife." There was more than just a little antiintellectualism in what the Cardinal was saying, an antiintellectualism that afflicted much of the Irish clergy in this century, and as a matter of fact the Cardinal was wrong; there were bishops and archbishops whose parents were college graduates. But aside from this, the Cardinal was saying that, given the same advantages and opportunities as the rich, the hierarchy, himself included, might have done anything that the rich had done. The rich held no terrors for Cardinal Cushing, although he was always considerate of them, and every year Joseph P. Kennedy quietly gave $1 million to the Archdiocese of Boston. Other Catholic institutions would compete for Kennedy's attention, but he would remain loyal to Cushing, and the other Catholic institutions would end up with consolation prizes such as Irene Dunne, say, or Rosalind Russell instead.

Sometimes a priest can meet the rich by dominating them, or, as the psychiatrists say, by infanticizing them. It is not necessarily a pernicious relationship, and in his years on the Atomic Energy Commission and as a likely political candidate, Thomas E. Murray, Jr., would make scarcely a public utterance until he had consulted with the theologian John Courtney Murray. The relationship was so close that when Thomas E. Murray, Jr., died, the theologian very nearly had a breakdown himself. Finally, a priest may get along with the rich folks by presenting himself as nothing more than a servant of God, as an intermediary, really, between Him and them, and as the tool for their salvation. This kind of priest can be a nuisance, filled as he is with the solemnity and righteousness of his calling, and usually he is found only in the homes of the guilty. A generation or so ago, the Irish were always feeling guilty about something or other, and so Father Killeen was always hanging around the Murrays and McDonnells.

Nonetheless, there are rewards to be found in the company of priests, and they need not be just the joys of fellowship or goodness. There can be a pious exhilaration about clerical company, too. The cardinals and bishops in Ireland, probably because they come from a long line of flagellants, have always found in the Irish church a purer and more self-sufficient form of Christianity than exists anywhere else, and over the years they have not looked at Rome with much awe. The Irish American hierarchy, however, has been different, seeing in Rome the Eternal City and moral authority, and its Irish American constituents have been much the same. The fine society that Cardinal O'Connell observed in Rome was made up mostly of Americans, and while the Cardinal barely suggested in his autobiography that its members were involved in papal politics, they almost certainly were because the princes of the church have always made up a fascinating aristocracy to Americans. In the 1920s and '30s, perhaps the most dedicated court follower was Mrs. Nicholas Brady, who was the daughter-in-law of the old patron of Thomas E. Murray. Mrs. Brady, who already owned a mansion called Inisfada on the North Shore of Long Island near Manhasset, decided to build a villa in Rome. It was called Casa del Sole, and through it passed the most eminent members of the Curia, including Eugenio Cardinal Pacelli. On hearing that the Cardinal enjoyed an occasional game of tennis, Mrs. Brady, who did not care much for the game herself, decided to have courts put in. She invited Pacelli to use them, and the Secretary of State for the Vatican did, going there as often as he could, and sometimes playing with Mr. Brady. Mrs. Brady, meanwhile, had met Father Francis J. Spellman, who was then a young priest assigned to the Secretariat of State. The story is that one day in St. Peter's Father Spellman noticed the Bradys sitting in back of him, while there were two empty seats in front of him. He saw to it that the Bradys got the better seats, and the grateful Mrs. Brady, on finding out his name, began to invite him to her villa, taking pains to do it when she knew that Cardinal Pacelli would also be there. The Cardinal knew Spellman slightly from the Secretariat of State, but their friendship did not really ripen until they were thrown together on the playing fields of Mrs. Brady.

In 1936, Cardinal Pacelli visited the United States. The Pope by then had made Mrs. Brady a Dame of Malta, allowing her to use the title Duchess, and the visit threw her into high excitement. Apparently, she hoped to more or less manage the Cardinal's trip, and although she was never able to quite do this, she called on Peter Grace of Grace Lines, Stanley Dollar of Dollar Lines, and Basil Harris of U.S. Lines to help her arrange things for His Eminence. They did, and Pacelli even stayed briefly at the Harris home in Rye, New York. He stayed even longer at Mrs. Brady's Inisfada, where so many people showed up to meet him that Mrs. Brady, beside herself in a dignified way, took to following him into the elevator, and then stalling it between floors so that she could get a word in, too. Eventually, Spellman, who was the Auxiliary Bishop of Boston, carried Pacelli off to Hyde Park for a

meeting with President Roosevelt, although Mrs. Brady got
him back again for a reception in her apartment at 910 Fifth
Avenue. The McDonnells, who lived on the floor above Mrs.
Brady, were at the reception, and to round things off nicely
one of their daughters later married a son of Basil Harris,
who, by now, was traveling around with the Cardinal. (Another of Harris' sons married a daughter of Thomas E. Murray, Jr.; the Irish Catholics moved in interlocking circles.) As
history shows, when Pacelli became Pope Pius XII one of his
first acts was to appoint Spellman Archbishop of New York.
Later he made him a cardinal. Through his friendship with
the Pope and his own consummate skills as a politician,
Cardinal Spellman was then very nearly able to choose the
other members of the hierarchy himself. Priests spoke of the
"Spellmanization" of the church, and "Spellie's boys," as they
were called, were everywhere. None of it would have happened, of course, without Mrs. Brady.

Nevertheless, Spellman himself was not particularly well
known when he arrived in New York. Besides, unlike most
members of the Irish American hierarchy, he did not look
particularly imposing, appearing to most people who met him
for the first time rather like a middle-aged cherub. "I never
come up to expectations," he said, although this did not stop
the high Irish in New York for a moment. Anna McDonnell
organized a reception for him at the Metropolitan Opera
House, and to her family's great surprise made a speech of
welcome from the stage. The next day, Al Smith, wearing the
splendid uniform of a papal chamberlain, visited the chancery,
and the new Archbishop was on his way. He had inherited an
Archdiocese that was made up of all New York City except
the boroughs of Brooklyn and Queens, and included the
counties of Westchester, Putnam, Dutchess, Orange, Rock-
land, Sullivan, and Ulster. It was $28 million in debt, and,
Cardinal O'Connell's superciliousness aside, the times really

did demand a priest who was something of a bookkeeper. In the twenty-eight years that Spellman was in New York the Archdiocese would spend more than $500 million on construction alone, and from the beginning Spellman would lean heavily on his Irish laity for advice about it. John Burke, the president of B. Altman & Company, Harry Haggerty, the president of Metropolitan Life, and John Coleman, a former president of the Stock Exchange, became his closest counselors, and among the other high Irish they became known as "The Blessed Trinity," ready to help Cardinal Spellman whenever they could. Coleman, who had been a poor boy raised in Hell's Kitchen in Manhattan, even got to be known as something of a gray eminence. This was because New York politicians have always called the chancery "the powerhouse," although when questioned about it, the politicians, fearful of offending someone, tend to deny that they have as much as heard of the chancery. Still, in each administration at City Hall the chancery, or powerhouse, has at least one ambassador who makes the Cardinal's views known, and one of the pastimes among City Hall reporters and lesser politicians is to guess the identity of the ambassador. Under Spellman it was decided that it was Coleman, and because the chancery always had great political power attributed to it, Coleman had great political power attributed to him, too.

The truth was that in Spellman's time the chancery, which once was prodigal with its power in practical politics, was almost restrained. The time had passed when an Irish monsignor could stand up at the funeral of a Tammany Hall leader and read Jimmy Walker out of the Democratic Party, or when the secretary to Patrick Cardinal Hayes could tell reporters that the Cardinal himself had ordered the police to break up a meeting on birth control at Town Hall. Cardinal Spellman was reduced to less dramatic activities, and one unofficial but probably accurate count is that in the last eighteen years of his reign he mounted the pulpit of St. Patrick's Cathedral only four times to talk of things that disturbed him: three times he spoke of the dangers of Communism, and once he asked everyone to stay away from dirty movies.

Spellman certainly was not to the taste of all the high Irish, but he was to most of them, and in his way he reflected them quite well. He was a man of small kindnesses and random generosities, which they were, too, and he shared their sense of being at once superior and inferior to everyone else. He knew, for instance, that an Irish Catholic was as good as anyone else, and obviously a good deal closer to God than most, but the hardship was that not everyone seemed to know it. There were high Protestant circles of invincible ignorance that excluded Catholics in general, and Irish Catholics in particular, and so the game among the Irish Catholics was to form their own circles, and then to exclude the Protestants. The Irish Catholics did not quite put it in those terms, and if they talked about it at all, which they seldom did because of their vanity, they spoke only of the pleasures of being with one's own and of protecting the faith. They did not say to one another that they wanted to be in some of those Protestant circles, or even that they resented being kept out. No, it was better to ignore the slights, and then to strike back in some refined way, some way with tone to it; this was something they understood. It was best of all for them when they could make their own rules for the game and then use their religion to sanctify them. That way they could be both moral and exclusive and still find a way of having everything the Protestants had.

Now, one thing the Protestants had were debutantes, and while the high Irish had plenty of girls they had few debutantes, the rules of becoming a debutante being fixed in such a way that few Irish Catholic girls could follow them. Traditionally, a girl became a debutante after her mother had be-

seeched a committee of elders to allow the girl to be presented
at their dance or cotillion. It was a tribal rite, a declaration
that the girl was now fully pubescent, and because it was tribal
the Irish Catholics never sat on the committees of elders, and
their girls never had a chance to be debutantes. At the Junior
Assemblies, for example, where every year young women
were presented to society, there were Catholic girls, but they
were almost always of the English or French persuasions,
never of the Irish kind. The Irish girls, even the ones from the
Sacred Heart convents, which were so exclusive that many of
them wouldn't accept the daughters of divorced parents, simply didn't make it.

Consequently, Anna McDonnell and Marie Murray had an
idea. The Irish Catholics would hold their own dances and
present the very best of their girls, not only to society, but to
Cardinal Spellman, too. The money that was raised would go
to the New York Foundling Hospital, and the dances would
be held just across from the Waldorf at Louis Sherry, which
was where Irish Catholics always went when they were feeling
very grand. There would be tea dances for the adolescents in
the afternoon, and then in the evening the older girls, escorted
by young men from Fordham, or, even better, Georgetown,
would make their debuts. Spellman saw the wisdom of the
idea at once, and that was how the Gotham Ball was born.
Chicago had something like it in the Chicago Debutante Cotillion, which was held at the same time as the elegant Passavant Cotillion, and was sponsored by the Frank J. Lewis Milk
Fund. Mrs. Lewis was one of the true grandes dames of the
church, and heavy with religious medals and jewelry, wrapped
in a white mink stole, and with the reigning Cardinal of the
Chicago Archdiocese on her right, she would receive the
debutantes. The Gotham, however, was classier than that,
and no one person would ever dominate it, although over the
years there would be battles and greatly bruised feelings over

the question of which girls were eligible for it. In this respect, despite the benevolent presence of the Cardinal, the Gotham Ball was just like any other debutantes' party, and so seriously was it sometimes taken that there are Irish Catholic ladies today who are just barely civil to other Irish Catholic ladies because of arguments over the Gotham ten and fifteen years ago. A former *New York Times* society reporter, himself Irish, and with a monsignor for an uncle, recalls the Gotham and its Protestant rival, the Junior Assemblies, this way:

"One night I'd be at the Gotham and the next night I'd be at the Junior Assemblies. The difference you wouldn't believe. The Irish kids at the Gotham would come in all polished and scrubbed within an inch of their lives, looking like they were modeling for the top of a wedding cake, for God's sake. Spellie would be sitting and smiling at everyone, and the kids would look so solemn and respectable you'd think they were training to be pall bearers. Then, at the Junior Assemblies, these Ivy League kids would come in looking like they'd just gotten out of bed. So help me, some of them would be wearing sweat socks with their tuxedos. They couldn't have cared less."

As a celebrity for the rich Irish Catholics, the only man who touched Cardinal Spellman was Fulton J. Sheen. Other celebrated priests came and went, like Father Payton of Ireland, who got $50,000 each year from Peter Grace of Grace Lines to spread a devotion to the rosary, or Father Keller, who got $50,000 a year from Mr. Grace for the Christophers. None, however, had the durability of Bishop Sheen, whose admirers over the years were legion, and whose detractors, it sometimes seemed, were nearly so. "A fascinating man infatuated by his own ego . . . Sheen is a consummate egocentric, a skillful actor who mesmerizes audiences," the Reverend D. P. Noonan wrote. "He is a kind of Everett Dirksen, playing all sides of an issue to suit the mood and time of his needs."

Noonan, who was once an assistant to Bishop Sheen, also said that Sheen's career was stopped by his lack of "submission to the will of the late Cardinal Spellman of New York." Sheen himself, on giving up his diocese in Rochester, New York, in 1969 said: "I could have gone higher and higher in the church, but I refused to pay the price." He did not explain what he meant, but then he hardly had to. The sophisticated Irish, who had been following his career from the start, knew all about it. In 1934, four years after Sheen had entered broadcasting on "The Catholic Hour" over NBC, Pius XI made him a papal chamberlain, with the title of Very Reverend Monsignor. A year after that, Pius XI made him a domestic prelate, with the title of Right Reverend Monsignor. This was a few years after Spellman had begun making his first moves up the hierarchy, and it ought to have been clear to everyone that sooner or later two such imperious men in the same organization would have problems with one another. Both knew Cardinal Pacelli before he became Pope Pius XII, but Spellman knew him first and better, and that was the difference. Still, Sheen made all those famous converts, not only Henry Ford, but also Clare Booth Luce, Heywood Broun, and the Communist Louis Budenz, and he was national director of the Society for the Propagation of the Faith, which raised millions for missionary enterprises, and in the 1950s he became one of the most striking television personalities of his time. He was always striking, and a Murray girl remembers that when he visited her convent in the 1930s, appearing in the doorway in white taffeta robes with a scarlet lining, the convent had been overcome by genteel hysteria. A Medici prince, the Murray girl thought, he looks like a Medici prince. In 1951, Pope Pius XII made Sheen a bishop, and at the same time an auxiliary bishop to Cardinal Spellman. Among the high Irish there was speculation that Sheen would also become a cardinal and eventually a member of the Curia, and they took to keeping a scorecard on him, especially in the competition with Spellman. For instance, Sheen had a private audience with the Pope every year, but then Spellman had one, too, and everyone knew that Cardinal Spellman would see the Pope as soon as he arrived in Rome and not be kept waiting at all. Ah, yes, the game would go on, but the Pope calls Sheen by his first name. Aha, the comeback would be, the Cardinal is the only one who knows the Pope well enough to give him gifts — why, last Christmas he gave him an electric razor. Usually, the argument ended there.

Some of the Irish were never entirely certain about Sheen. They suspected his mannerisms, and when he was in the fullness of his television career they looked a little skeptical and called him "Uncle Fultie," although they did it without derision, and more often than not they said he was "a holy man." The Irish are the last Americans to use the word holy without being self-conscious about it, and when they say it they mean prayerful and godly. The rich said it often about Sheen, and the rich were attracted to him. The first had been Thomas Farrell, the coal and iron man who had paid for Sheen's education in Belgium, and when Farrell's son married Mary Cavanagh and took her on a honeymoon Sheen went with them. Anna McDonnell had discovered Sheen on the trip to Lourdes, and when Clare Booth Luce embraced Catholicism, Sheen suggested to her that Anna McDonnell be her godmother. Everything was en famille, and every Christmas Eve Sheen would leave his rectory and visit the McDonnells' apartment. Some time after dinner, when the children were all engaged in their own amusements, Anna McDonnell would walk the hallways saying, "Get ready, get ready." Then the children would assemble in the living room, and Sheen would practice his Christmas sermon on them. A little later they would hear it again in church.

While the McDonnells had Sheen all those years, Thomas E. Murray, Jr., and his family had a slow procession of Jesuits winding in and out of their lives. When one of Murray's sons found himself spending two years in the freshman class at Jesuit Georgetown, unable to pass quite enough subjects to get out of it, the Jesuits said that it was all right, and then let him go on for another year. His father, they said, was a nice man.

Lester Cuddihy, Julia Murray's husband, liked to have priests around, too, but Cuddihy, who for a while was the only Catholic member of the Players Club, thought of himself as an iconoclast and felt he should argue with them, or at least occasionally bait them in a mild way. Like his brother-in-law Jack Murray, Cuddihy was bored with the sermons of Father Killeen, although his children were never allowed to criticize them in the slightest. That was not the Irish Catholic way in those days, and to the clergy one was supposed to show a generosity of both spirit and purse. One day, for example, a Brother Hurley knocked on the door of the Cuddihys' house in Water Mill. He had been wandering around, looking for a place where some Irish Christian Brothers could spend their vacations. He did not know Cuddihy, and it was only chance that had brought them together. Cuddihy invited him in, and showed him the house, the pool, the dock, the eleven acres of elegant lawn, the poolroom, and the squash and tennis courts. Enchanting, Brother Hurley said. I'm glad you like it, Lester Cuddihy said. Then he said that he and his wife and children would move out, and that Brother Hurley and his thirty Irish Christian Brothers could move in. They did, and they kept returning for ten years. When Lester Cuddihy died in 1953, choking on a chicken bone that caught in his throat on a July Fourth day in Southampton, Julia Cuddihy decided that she did not want to stay in the house without him, and she gave the house and all its property to the local bishop. She hoped, she said, that it would be used as a convent for nuns who would pray for her family. The Bishop, however, had a slightly different idea, and instead of nuns some monks moved in. Later, the house and property were sold to a developer, but Julia Cuddihy said not a word, and it would have been out of character if she had. The year after her husband died, and three years after one of her sons had been stricken by polio and was now living in her apartment in an iron lung, Mrs. Cuddihy felt the need for a rest. It happened to be the beginning of Lent, and she chose to go to Palm Beach. She had always given up the pleasure of a solitary cocktail before dinner for Lent, but this year, feeling that the sadnesses were too great, she thought that she might keep the cocktail. At confession, she asked a priest about it, but the priest said no. If she were going to Palm Beach, he said, then the sadnesses would be behind her, and she wouldn't really need the cocktail. Mrs. Cuddihy could not be disobedient, but she appealed to her daughter, who, in turn, appealed to an old Paulist named Mc-Sorley. "My child," he said, "I cannot send word to your mother to just drink. So tell her I approve whatever any good doctor would recommend." Any good doctor, of course, would tell Julia Cuddihy to have her drink. One did, and greatly relieved, Mrs. Cuddihy departed for Palm Beach.

In the winter of 1976, Julia Cuddihy, who was then eighty years old, was living in an apartment at 88th Street and Park Avenue. The building had St. Thomas More to the north and St. Ignatius Loyola to the south, and it was greatly favored by other Irish Catholics, although Mrs. Cuddihy, who was seriously ill, could enjoy few of its consolations. Years before she had suffered a heart attack, and then she had been stricken by Parkinson's disease, and her doctors had forbidden her to go to Mass. Instead, a priest would visit her every day. Nonetheless, Mrs. Cuddihy was worried, and so every day from her bed or her wheelchair she would ask the priest if it was truly all right that she did not go to Mass. The priest would say that it was, and Julia Cuddihy would say, Well, if you're sure, and she would smile and feel greatly relieved, and then perhaps go back to sleep.

VII

Aristocrats at Last

THE OLD BROOKLYN *Eagle* caught the spirit of the thing quite nicely; under a headline that said, PLEBEIAN EYES POP AS ELITE SWOOP ON SOUTHAMPTON, it reported that "the marital merger may be said to rival that of Wallis Simpson and the Duke of Windsor." Since the Duke was once the King of England, the *Eagle* was being excessive, but the summer of 1940 was full of whimsy, and the *Eagle*'s seizure was understandable. The wedding of Anne McDonnell was of interest, not only to the society editors, but to a large part of the country, and among the McDonnells, Murrays, and Cuddihys it set off complicated and sometimes simultaneous feelings of envy, pride, grandeur, and disdain.

Anne and her family had gone to Europe on the maiden voyage of the *Normandie* in 1935, and returning to America aboard the *Queen Mary* they had met Mr. and Mrs. Edsel Ford and their son, Henry. Anne and Henry were both eighteen, and Henry was smitten instantly. Anne, however, was not much interested in him, or at least that was what she kept saying, and the possibility is that if it had not been for Anna McDonnell, the romance might not have survived the Atlantic crossing. Henry, who was a student at Yale, began coming down from New Haven to visit the McDonnells, and sometimes he would do it solely on Anna McDonnell's invitation. "Not Henry Ford again," Anne would complain, and once, when she had been asked to join the Fords for a week's cruise on their yacht and a cousin had said how marvelous she thought that was, Anne had turned in amazement. "A week with Henry Ford!" she said. "How can anyone spend a week with Henry Ford?" The fact was that many young women would have done it with the deepest of pleasure, and in the family Anne's reluctance was considered a little odd. She was not considered the comeliest of the McDonnell girls, and for years her father had grumbled to her about her weight, saying she would never find a husband unless she lost some. Still, Henry did keep coming around, and he did propose, and on the night that he did Anne went home and found her mother waiting with iced champagne. Nonetheless, there were problems, and the largest by far was religion. Henry was a Methodist, and when he asked James McDonnell for his daughter's hand, Mr. McDonnell said that Anne could never marry anyone but a Catholic. Henry by then would do anything to marry Anne, just as years later he would do anything to divorce her, and so he agreed to become a Catholic. Monsignor Fulton J. Sheen was invited to instruct Henry in the mysteries of the faith, although this left Father Keller of the Christophers a little put out because as another old friend of the family's, he had wanted to do the same thing. The next Easter, Henry Ford went to St. Patrick's Cathedral, where he attended Mass in public for the first time, and on July 13, the day before he married Anne, he was baptized. Fulton Sheen did it at the Church of the Sacred Hearts in Southampton, and this time Father Killeen was a little put out. He had wanted to do it, too.

The wedding was perfect. The McDonnells were determined that the Fords would know who they were, and so they summoned two bishops to assist Monsignor Sheen at the ceremony, hired sixteen private detectives to guard the wedding gifts, and rented a couple of buses to take the bridesmaids to church standing up so their dresses wouldn't wrinkle. The organist from St. Patrick's Cathedral came to play, and in honor of the occasion he composed three new pieces. Much of the pomp, however, was lost on the Fords, who for years had worked hard at keeping their names out of the papers, and whose idea of a proper family evening was to have Edsel Ford read the Bible aloud. The grandfather, old Henry Ford, had his various eccentricities, one of which was to insist that his grandson Henry eat a handful of grass now and then, but by and large the Ford pleasures were simple ones. Moreover, young Henry believed in all the old amenities, and before he and Anne decided on a wedding date he solemnly asked Anne's older sister, Catherine, who was also engaged, if it would be all right if he and Anne were married first. Henry was that kind of man, conscious of family, and given to grand gestures, and there would come a time when some members of the family could not handle it all. Even in 1940, amid the signs of jubilation by the golden boys and girls, there was a glimmer of something else, something they could not define, or clearly feel. It was a hint of discord, a touch of envy, or perhaps the awareness that for years to come they would be identified as the brother- or sister-in-law of Henry Ford, or as the cousin of the lady who married him. This would be gratifying, lending their names a certain distinction and flair, but also introducing something unmanageable into their lives. They would become captives of their image, and never really escape it. James McDonnell, the father of the bride, was a hard little man, with a great dome of a forehead and a deep respect for money. Ordinarily, he was not much given to reflection, but on the night before his daughter married Henry Ford he made a solemn pronouncement to one of his other children. "The marriage," he said, "is the worst thing that could happen to this family."

Nevertheless, the day itself was splendid, James McDonnell

beamed, and a reporter wrote that he was "gay and disarm-
ing." Old Henry Ford and his wife had arrived the day before
in their private railroad car, which was attached to the Can-
nonball, the fastest train on Long Island, and when Ford got
there he said that he remembered meeting Anne's grandfather
at an assembly of Consolidated Edison almost forty years before. Mr. and Mrs. Edsel Ford arrived on the *Onika,* their
yacht, and Rose Kennedy and her sons John and Joseph and
her daughters Eunice and Kathleen, who was to be a bridesmaid, came out by limousine. "If you ask me," said a lady
who did not particularly like the McDonnells, "this is just the
B. Altman crowd." She meant that except for the Fords, the
Firestones, the Edisons, and maybe a few others, the guests
were mostly New York Irish with no particular distinction
besides their money. The lady, who was New York Irish herself, was put down as a sorehead. Cholly Knickerbocker began his column all in capitals that day by proclaiming that
SOUTHAMPTON WAS EN FETE, and then he scored something
of a scoop by printing a list of all the organ selections. The
Daily News ran a picture of the wedding on page one, and in
its story said that Anne's grandfather had left a fortune of
somewhere between $35 and $50 million, which was far more
than he had, but which rather pleased the Murrays and Mc-
Donnells when they read it the next day. Anne was curiously
unsmiling in nearly all the wedding pictures, and watching her
walk down the aisle that day, her face almost lowered into a
bouquet of white orchids, one of her sisters had wondered
what she was thinking. Throughout her engagement, Anne
had been dating an Irish boy from Southampton, and the night
before she had sneaked out of the house to see him one last
time. "My God," the sister thought, "if mother or Henry
knew about that." Sheen, in purple robes with white vest-
ments, performed the high nuptial Mass, and then, departing
from the usual order of things, he preached a short sermon
about love. "Only when you promise to stake your eternal

salvation on your fidelity to one another will the church con-
sent to unite you as man and wife," he said. "Your life thus
becomes bonded at the foot of the altar, sealed with the seal of
the Cross, and signed with the red sign of the Eucharist."
Someone noticed that it was exactly 12:48 when Sheen
paused, smiled, and with a nice sense of the dramatic said,
"Pope Pius XII sends his apostolic blessing on Mr. and Mrs.
Henry Ford the Second."

Then it was over. The organist played Mendelssohn's Wedding March, the mothers of both the bride and groom began to
cry, and Anne seemed to manage her first tight smile. The
wedding party and 1000 guests went back to the McDonnells'
cottage, and the Sheriff of Riverhead, worried that someone
might try to pinch the wedding gifts, sent two Irish deputies to
help the private detectives stand guard. The McDonnells had
put up a huge tent with a ceiling of blue silk over a polished
wooden floor, and all about they had hung silver vases with
red roses. They had also put porcelain sailboats with baby
calla lilies in them on the tables, and the effect, everyone said,
was lovely. When Anne and Henry finally sat down after
standing in the reception line and posing for photographers,
the band began to play, and Henry took Anne on the dance
floor. Her father cut in, inspiring the band to play "My Heart
Belongs to Daddy," and then Edsel Ford cut in. Anne's
brother James cut in on him, and then old Henry Ford, after
telling the band to play a waltz, cut in on James. Thin, bent
over, the tails of his cutaway flying behind him, the man who
had known her grandfather forty years before moved Anne
round and about with quick, hopping steps. Everyone else
cleared off the floor and applauded, and a bridesmaid, moved
nearly beyond words, glanced at young Henry standing in
back, and then leaned across the young man sitting next to her
and spoke to the bridesmaid on his right. "Can you imagine,"
she said, "being Mrs. Henry Ford?"

On that day, at least, there was something like awe at this

final triumph of the Irish, and to catch it in its full and heady flavor it is best to return one more time to the story in the Brooklyn *Eagle*. It was written by a lady named Cogan. "Seldom has there been such a joyous wedding reception," she wrote, "such a setting, right smack on the ocean, like a movie scene; such a gracious young couple, who romped all over the grounds enjoying every minute of the fun; such a spontaneous gaiety of guests and such mingling of classes; such fruit of the vine, magnum after magnum of Roederer; such a delicious wedding breakfast; such a genuine democratic spirit. The cook's family hobnobbed with millionaires; Henry Ford and Al Smith laughed at each other's jokes; the McDonnell baby, five-year-old Sean, played with the priests, of which there were dozens; Monsignor Sheen sipped soft drinks and the chauffeur's son had his first taste of champagne." Now, if the cook's family did much hobnobbing it was because they had slipped away from the tent set up for the staff in the polo field, and if the chauffeur's son had any champagne he probably had swiped it. But these were small things, and the truth was that Anna and James McDonnell had produced a successful wedding and that it had been attended by an enormous amount of publicity. Anne and Henry went to Hawaii on their honeymoon, and when they got there Anne wrote a letter to her mother. "I guess they'll know who we are now," she said. It was the cry of an Irish girl who had finally made it.

In big families, the first child to get married often inspires the other children to do the same, and after Anne there was a procession of her sisters, brothers, and cousins to the altar. Rosamund Murray, a daughter of Joseph and Theresa Murray, married Buckley Byers in the ceremony that Thomas E. Murray, Jr., refused to go to, and then Mary Jane Cuddihy married James MacGuire. Catherine McDonnell married R. Peter Sullivan; Marie Murray, a daughter of Thomas E.

Murray, Jr., married Basil Harris, Jr.; and Patricia Murray, a daughter of Jack and Jeanne Murray, married Jeffrey Roche. Wedding followed wedding in no particular order, and until some of the unions began to fly apart a few years later there was not much reason to think that this generation would be any different in its marital proclivities than the one that had gone before it. For one thing, in these first marriages in the new generation, there was the suitability of the spouses, most of whom were from respectable Irish Catholic families; and if they were not Irish Catholic they were certainly respectable. Buckley Byers may have been a Protestant, but he was also coxswain of the Yale crew that Henry Ford managed, and his mother was descended from Robert Morris, who signed the Declaration of Independence, and his brother had married into the Grace family. That family, if not the last word in Irish Catholic piety and wealth, was very close to it. James MacGuire, who married Mary Jane Cuddihy, was the grand-son of James Butler, who, when he died in 1934, left behind him the Butler stores, a racing stable, and a considerable amount of money. Butler's generosity was responsible for the founding of Marymount School and College in Tarrytown, New York, and in 1926 he had bought the old Burden house on Fifth Avenue and 84th Street and given it to Marymount so it would have a New York outlet. Peter Sullivan, who married Catherine McDonnell, was the son of a doctor who for years was the only Catholic associated with the Mayo Clinic. Then he became the personal physician to Patrick Cardinal Hayes, whereupon he always sat in the first pew in St. Patrick's Cathedral on Sundays. His father before him had been a doctor, whose wife had arranged flowers on the altar of St. Gregory's in Brooklyn with Thomas E. Murray's wife. Basil Harris, Jr., who married Marie Murray, was a son of the man who escorted Cardinal Pacelli on his tour of America and who just before his death gave millions to the Archdiocese of

New York. Jeffrey Roche, who married Patricia Murray, was the grandson of James Jeffrey Roche, who was born in Ireland, found his way to Boston, and succeeded the celebrated John Boyle O'Reilly as editor of *The Pilot,* the leading Catholic journal in America. He wrote poetry and biography, loved Ireland, and became something of a hero to Catholic intellectuals. His son, Arthur Somers Roche, wrote short stories and novels about life among the rich, and when Howard Chandler Christy illustrated one of them he chose a girl called Jeanne Durand to model for him. She married Jack Murray, and it was their daughter Patricia who married Jeffrey, the son of Arthur Somers Roche.

Obviously, the marriages were being made within comfortable and circumscribed circles, with partners who did not represent much in the way of the unexpected. The only unexpected thing was that Murrays, McDonnells, and Cuddihys did not marry into some of the families that everyone expected them to marry into. "It's funny," Joseph P. Kennedy once said to a Murray girl, "all of us and all of you, and no marriages between us." There never was a marriage, although once or twice there did seem to be a chance at one. Charlotte McDonnell and John F. Kennedy went together for a while, but then Charlotte decided to marry a son of Basil Harris'. The decision was eased, she said, when Kennedy, on duty with PT–109, confused two envelopes and sent her the letter he had intended to send to a girl in Hollywood. Later, Charlotte's sister Marjorie went out with John Kennedy, but he was less interested in her than Robert Kennedy was. That never got anyplace, either.

If anyone in the family was going to step outside the circumscribed circle and do something outrageous, then it was inevitable that the first one to do it would be a child of Jack Murray's. His children had always stood apart from their cousins, although they had never known quite why, but the fact was that the family had never forgiven Jack and Jeanne for getting married in the first place. As the years went on the resentment had grown, become calcified, and shown itself in the small meannesses and enduring spites that the Irish in large families are so good at inflicting on one another. When all the Murrays and McDonnells were living virtually next door to one another in Southampton, Thomas E. Murray, Jr., had suggested to both his own and the McDonnells' children that they have as little as possible to do with Jack and Jeanne's children. Anna McDonnell had supported him in this cruel decision, although her husband, James, apparently had reservations about it, and he told her once that one day she would be sorry about all of it. Nevertheless, Thomas E. Murray, Jr., and Anna McDonnell persisted, and the sins of Jack and Jeanne Murray were visited on their children, and there was, Thomas E. Murray, Jr., and Anna McDonnell seemed to think, no end to the wicked things those children might one day do. In the parameters of their world they were absolutely right, and on December 12, 1945, their worst suspicions were confirmed. One of Jack Murray's daughters did something truly unpardonable: she married Alfred Gwynne Vanderbilt.

Vanderbilt, as all the world was reminded in the papers the next day, was a sportsman, a war hero, a millionaire many times over, and a great socialite. He was also divorced, having once been married to the niece of the man who owned Seabiscuit, and if he professed any religious belief at all it had escaped public notice. Jeanne, his new bride, had been an actress, a model, and a nicely brought up Irish Catholic girl, who, while young, had hung a picture of Alfred Vanderbilt on her wall the way other girls her age had hung a picture of Gable, say, or Cary Grant. When they finally did meet, Jeanne was a press agent at the Stork Club, and Alfred was 130 pounds of insouciant charm. From the beginning it was certain that he would propose and that she would accept, and the problem, she thought, would be telling her mother about it. "If he asks you to marry him, you say yes," said Ed Flynn, who was Democratic boss of the Bronx, as well as an old family friend. "I'll take care of your mother." So, Alfred proposed, Jeanne accepted, and Ed Flynn spoke to her mother. Actually, it was a fait accompli. Not wanting to embarrass her mother or sisters by asking them to attend the ceremony, and knowing that she would catch hell from the rest of the family anyway, Jeanne had eloped. She and Alfred had flown to Philadelphia in a small plane, and in the air Jeanne Murray had been possessed by a single thought. "We will crash," she told herself. "I am marrying out of the church, and so we will crash." Nonetheless, she and Alfred survived, and they were married by a magistrate, while another judge was best man. When he heard about it, Thomas E. Murray, · Jr., overcoming his old dislike for Jeanne's mother, rushed to her side to commiserate. She was sick with the flu, and in her bedroom that night he proposed a course of action. An annulment, he said, we must try for an annulment. There was no annulment, and so there came down on the new Mrs. Vanderbilt anger, scorn, and all the sullen rage of the betrayed Irish. Priests wrote to her, demanding to know how a girl from such a nice family could do so wicked a thing, and one of her cousins, a girl she had always liked, wrote to say that now she would burn in hell. Uncle Tom, Jeanne thought, must have gotten her to write it. That winter, the Vanderbilts moved to Beverly Hills because Alfred's horses were racing at Santa Anita. Jeanne went to a priest in Beverly Hills to ask him how she could get right with the church, and the priest said there was only one thing she could do; she must leave her husband. The next Sunday Jeanne went to Mass. She would not take communion, of course, knowing that she was not in what was called a state of grace, but she could sit and listen. The priest she had spoken to only a few days before preached a homily on fallen women, especially those who had been suborned by famous names. One of the most notorious cases, he said, his voice full of sanctimonious anger, was that of Jeanne Vanderbilt. Since the Irish hardly ever made things easy on themselves, and since Jeanne was stricken with guilt anyway, she returned to the same church the next Sunday, and for all the Sundays she stayed in Beverly Hills.

The next summer, the Vanderbilts went to Southampton, and walking one day on the beach they saw Anna and James McDonnell. They were staring at the ocean, and they did not see the Vanderbilts until they were almost beside them. The McDonnells looked, and then with great deliberation they turned their backs and stared once more at the ocean. They would not recognize their niece and her husband, although their oldest daughter would. This was Catherine, who was standing a little apart from her parents. Haltingly, and with an embarrassed smile, she said, "Hello, Jeanne." It was a kindness that Jeanne remembered for years. One winter, Alfred having forsaken Santa Anita for the Florida tracks, the Vanderbilts were in Palm Beach. Father Keller came to lecture there at the Four Arts Society, and Mrs. Vanderbilt, knowing him as an old family friend, wanted to invite him to tea. She left a note at his hotel, asking him to visit, and he answered with a note saying he would not. For him to have tea with the Vanderbilts, he said, would mean that he approved of their marriage.

So, Mrs. Vanderbilt was bereft of the consolations of the clergy and much of her family, but her life was not all bad, and there were certain pleasures in being Mrs. Vanderbilt. For one, there was Broadhollow, the estate that Alfred bought near Old Westbury, Long Island. It had a graceful Georgian mansion, with ten master bedrooms, an uncounted number of fireplaces, and a dining room that was circular at one end and opened up onto a garden. The mansion faced

110 acres of lawn and more gardens, and it had a staff of twelve during the week and fifteen on weekends, and that did not include the six men who worked to keep up the 110 acres. It is not absolutely sure that the very rich are different, no matter what Fitzgerald said, but it is certain that they do things that other people don't. The Vanderbilts, for example, were friends with their neighbors John Hay Whitney and his wife, Betsey, and William S. Paley and his wife, Babe. Whitney owned the *Herald Tribune* and other things, and Paley owned the Columbia Broadcasting System. Together they all enjoyed the small pleasures of watching new movies in Paley's living room, or playing softball on Whitney's front lawn, while his butlers stood by with iced drinks on silver trays. The Vanderbilts did not show movies or hold sporting contests, although their old house in Maryland had its own bowling alley, but they did entertain. They entertained former kings, old generals, retired presidents, and a great many movie stars at Broadhollow, and when they took a cottage at the Beverly Hills Hotel, or a house at Saratoga, they would entertain there, too.

On weekends at Saratoga, if Alfred did not have a horse running, the Vanderbilts would retreat to Margaret Emerson's lodge in the Adirondacks. Mrs. Emerson, or Ma Emerson, as everyone called her, was Alfred's mother. After his father went down on the *Lusitania* in 1915 and left her with a considerable amount of money, Ma had three more husbands, none of whom died dramatically, and all of whom had to be divorced. Alfred had a full brother, a half-brother, and a half-sister, but Ma was sometimes careless about family relationships, and so Alfred did not meet his half-brother until 1936, when he was introduced to him at a party. The full brother jumped from a hotel window, and the half-sister found her own private sorrows in Florida. The half-brother, who was an issue from Alfred Vanderbilt Sr.'s first marriage, which was not to Ma, became the Governor of Rhode Island. Late in life, Ma Emerson embraced Catholicism, and once she took Jeanne to lunch with Cardinal Spellman at the chancery. The Cardinal was warm to Ma, who talked about giving the Archdiocese her Adirondack estate, but he did not seem to care for Jeanne. Of course, Jeanne had thought sourly, I married out of the church.

Nonetheless, Jeanne Vanderbilt persisted in the old faith, and after she had given birth to a girl, whom she called Heidi, she set about having her baptized. Alfred would have none of it, indeed would not even talk about it, and so accompanied only by her old nurse, who was now her baby's nurse, and feeling very much like one of her great-grandmothers must have felt when she was living under the Penal Laws, Mrs. Vanderbilt stole out to church and had Heidi baptized. This was in Maryland, and when the Vanderbilts moved to New York, Mrs. Vanderbilt gave birth to a boy, who was named after his father. Alfred still detested the idea of having a child of his baptized, and so once again Mrs. Vanderbilt, accompanied by the nurse, stole out of the house. She drove around, saw a small church that looked inviting, and on finding a young priest there she said that she wanted her baby baptized, and that his name was Alfred Gwynne Vanderbilt, Jr. The priest looked stunned, said he was not sure he could do it, was not sure that it could be done at all, and would she please come back the next day? Grown skeptical by now about the clergy and its ways, Mrs. Vanderbilt was absolutely sure that he could do it, that there was no way he could not do it, and that what he wanted to do was to tell his rector, who would tell the Bishop, who would pass the word on to the chancery that someone was bringing in a Vanderbilt to be baptized. This is exactly what did happen, and when Jeanne, the nurse, and the baby returned to the church, the young priest, now full of solicitude, said he had been wrong, and that certainly the infant could be baptized. "Yes, I thought he could be," Mrs. Vanderbilt said evenly, and wondered once again why the rich and the clergy always had to dance such an intricate gavotte.

If the clergy could be forgiving to a baby, one might expect some of the Murrays and McDonnells to be forgiving to an adult, and something very much like that happened to Mrs. Vanderbilt. Her mother began to show up for longer and longer weekends at Broadhollow; her brothers and sisters came, too, and the rest of the family, who were now being identified as the cousins, brothers, or sisters of both Mrs. Ford and Mrs. Vanderbilt, began to show some grace. Mrs. Vanderbilt was extraordinarily beautiful, and there was always something in the papers about her comings and goings. At Saratoga one year, when a reporter asked her about the hat she was wearing and she said she had picked it up at a hat bar for only $4.95, the Associated Press, thinking this was quixotic, carried a photograph of Jeanne in her hat, and the photograph appeared, it seemed, nearly everywhere. Jeanne apparently was making a good thing of her life, probably even enjoying it, and while it was certain that she would fry in hell for marrying Alfred, it would have made it easier on some of the Murrays and McDonnells if she had begun to show a little discomfort now. Besides, she was only the daugher of Jack and Jeanne Murray, who never had all that much money, and now she seemed to have such a lot of it. It was all so unfair, and who did she think she was, anyway?

Nonetheless, there did come a time when Mrs. Vanderbilt was not particularly happy; her marriage was breaking up. It was not doing so in a dramatic way; instead, it was eroding, which is the way it is with most marriages that fail. Jeanne and Alfred never had much to talk about when they were alone, and as the marriage went on the silences grew longer. Alfred would take trips to Europe or Africa or wherever his fancy led him, and he would not take Jeanne. This was unhealthy, although it was not intolerable, but it did become difficult when he showed up in other places, in Saratoga or Paris, for example, with other women. Irish Catholic ladies did not break up their marriages easily, and so the other women were also not intolerable to Jeanne, although Alfred's habit of talking about them was. He spoke often of his conquests, and even though some of them seemed imaginary, this did become intolerable.

Eventually, Jeanne told Alfred Vanderbilt she was leaving him, and after staying in her room and crying for two days and two nights, she did. He went to Africa; she went away with the children, and when she and the children returned and a reporter heard about the separation, he called her about it. "I'll call you back," she said, and then got in touch with Frank Conniff, the Hearst newspaperman, who had married her sister Liz. Conniff said that she might as well get it over with and tell the reporter that she and Alfred had separated. She did, and this was a mistake because in 1955 the news about a Vanderbilt's marriage breaking up was thought to be as good a story as one about a Vanderbilt's getting married. The reporters descended into the lobby and onto the street outside the Vanderbilts' apartment and stayed there. One day, two days, and on her way out of the building on the third day Mrs. Vanderbilt asked a reporter how long he thought the vigil would go on. "About a week," he said with the measured guess of a professional, "and then it will all die down." This seemed too long to Mrs. Vanderbilt, and she removed herself to Babe and Bill Paley's house and hid out. She was beginning a legal separation, that time before a divorce when lawyers battle one another over the size of the settlement, and it was then that she grew close to Anthony Nutting, who had been the British Ambassador to the United Nations, and was now the Minister of State for Foreign Affairs. He was thirty-five years old, handsome, and the heir to both a lot of money and the baronetcy that had been created in Dublin for his grandfather, who had sold whiskey. Moreover, he was also supposed to be Prime Minister Anthony Eden's choice as his successor, and when Eden heard that Nutting was seeing Mrs. Vanderbilt he became distressed. She was not yet divorced, and Eden, fearing a scandal, lectured Nutting and then wrote letters, warning him about "that lady in question." Nutting saw her, anyway. Then, when Britain and France attacked Egypt in the small war over the Suez Canal, Nutting resigned as Minister of State and said he was doing it to protest the attack. The people who are supposed to know about these things, however, said he had resigned to be with Jeanne. A columnist in the *Daily News* hedged on it this way:

> Has Venus rather than Mars won out as a dominating influence in the affairs of England's political glamor boy, Anthony Nutting? Members of international society are certain that is so. The Rt. Hon. Anthony Nutting has just resigned as Minister of State for Foreign Affairs. This is in protest against Britain's war on Egypt. Exit Mars! Now enter Venus: Nutting is believed committed to the idea of marrying a beautiful American — Mrs. Alfred G. Vanderbilt.

It remained for the authoritative Cholly Knickerbocker to set matters straight. Under a headline that said, NUTTING VENTURED, NUTTING GAINED, the old arbiter wrote:

> Some people, of course, tried to connect Nutting's resignation with his forthcoming divorce and plans to marry the soon-to-be divorced wife of Alfred G. Vanderbilt. But there is no truth whatever in that story. The Nutting decision was not for romantic but for political reasons exclusively.

Tony Nutting and Jeanne Vanderbilt continued to see each other, but they never got married, even though Jeanne got her divorce. After the divorce, Jeanne still felt oppressed in her soul, and so she went to a priest. He was a distinguished Jesuit, who had been the president of Fordham University, and forever after Jeanne would remember him as a cold man. She asked him what she could do to make things right with God and the church, and quickly he said, "Ten years' penance." Thinking that there must be another way, Jeanne got up, left, and went back into the world again.

The marriage of Anne and Henry Ford lasted longer than that of Jeanne and Alfred Vanderbilt, and the erosion took longer. Among other things, there was a matter of taste. Henry's life was in Detroit, where at the age of twenty-eight he became head of the Ford Motor Company; Anne hated Detroit. "Why, dear, you look lovely," Mrs. Edsel Ford said to her one night while they were having dinner at the McDonnells' apartment in New York. Mrs. Ford was not being arch, but she had noticed that Anne was wearing a dress. In Detroit, she wore skirts and sweaters most of the time. That place, she seemed to be saying, wasn't worth the effort of dressing up. Anne wanted to return to Southampton and the comfort of her family in the summers; Henry hated Southampton. They tried Palm Beach for a while, and then they went to Southampton. Henry thought Father Killeen was a bore, and here they compromised. Instead of Sacred Hearts, they went to Our Lady of Poland, which the family always called "the Polish church." Father Killeen never understood why they had left him. Henry said he wanted a traditional summer house, something modest. They bought land from the actor Richard Barthelmess, and on it they put up a big white palace. In the family, it was called Versailles. Still, Ford was a captain of industry, and he could not be expected to take Southampton lying down. One night, after a party at the Southampton Beach Club, he borrowed a lady's lipstick and with great care drew a mustache on a portrait of Newell

Tilton. Tilton, Cleveland Amory says, was "the last of the species once known as *arbiter elegantiarum,*" and among the stockbrokers at the Beach Club an *arbiter elegantiarum* was someone to be prized. The directors of the club said Henry Ford would be expelled from the membership unless he apologized, which he did, writing them a letter. (A few years ago, the directors did not approve a membership application from Mrs. Peter Lawford, the sister of President Kennedy. She was blackballed by a single vote, and that was cast by an Irish Catholic.)

There were other things that divided Anne and Henry Ford, and one of them was publicity. Anne enjoyed it; Henry did not, even though later in his life he would seem to court it. "I think publicity bothers Henry more than it does me," Anne said. This was after the *Ladies' Home Journal* and *Harper's Bazaar* had sent photographers through the Fords' mansion in Grosse Pointe, and Henry, not amused, had told his wife that it had better not happen again. Immediately afterward, there were full-page spreads on the Fords in the Detroit newspapers. Henry did not like that, either. He was complaining by now that Anne would not go with him when he went out to give the innumerable speeches he was making all over the country, and she, in turn, was complaining that he liked other women too much. At a cocktail party one night, Henry was sitting next to a pretty girl, talking to her, and on seeing them Anne rose up and turned her chair around so that her back was to them. The pretty girl asked a friend of the Fords' why she had done that, and the friend said that it was always this way. "She just won't look at Henry at parties," she said. Consequently, the grievances mounted between husband and wife, never growing truly serious, but introducing an intermittent sullenness into the marriage. At a party in the home of a movie producer, Henry was talking in one corner of the room, while Anne was looking at the producer's art collection in the other.

"Henry," she said loudly, "if you get off your fat ass and come over here you might learn something." Anne was developing an interest in art, as the rich often do, and sometimes she was imperious about it. When a French museum would not part with a picture she wanted for the house in Southampton, Anne seemed to regard it as a personal slight, and she complained bitterly about it to her brother Murray McDonnell. Murray, who would one day preside over the collapse of McDonnell & Company, the family business, was Anne's great confidant and adviser. Henry did not like that, either, and he complained about it, saying that if Anne did not stop asking Murray for advice instead of himself it would be the end of their marriage. All these things might not have meant much, and better marriages have suffered more, but then Henry met Mrs. Maria Christina Vettore Austin.

Mrs. Austin, who was called Christina, was a blond Italian of considerable charm and vitality, and she was divorced from a British businessman. She and Henry began a liaison that lasted five years, and in the best tradition of these things it was full of tears, recriminations, and misunderstandings. They would break up and come together again, and while Christina was living in Paris and Henry in Detroit they would talk on the telephone for five hours at a time. Sometimes she would doze off in the middle of the conversation. Now, there are few liaisons between men and women that remain liaisons, and ordinarily they turn into other things. When the intensity becomes great enough and it has gone on for a very long time, then there is almost nothing to do except to end the relationship entirely or else to sanctify it in marriage. Henry and Christina dithered, of course, because there is always dithering in relationships like theirs, and then they got married. It had not been easy, and toward the end Christina told Henry that it was all off, and that she could no longer stand any of it; she said that she wanted to be left alone. Then a friend of Henry's visited Christina, and then he saw Henry. "Henry," he said, "you're crazy if you don't marry her."

Anne and Henry were divorced in 1964, and until it happened Anne had seemed to feel that it could never happen. It was the way of Irish Catholics to believe that a marriage once solemnized could not end, but the center does not always hold, and things do get worse. Anne wept, raged, and threatened, and in the end she went to Sun Valley and got the divorce. When she did, the Diocese of Rockville Centre, in which her Southampton house was located, issued a curious statement saying that permission for a divorce is sometimes given when there is "grave cause." In the family, it was said that Anne's settlement was $20 million. The next year, Henry and Christina were married, and because they did they were both automatically excommunicated. Neither of them, however, has ever said a word about it.

There were other marriages and divorces, and other failures and successes among the grandchildren of Thomas E. Murray. Murray McDonnell married the daughter of Horace Flanigan, who was the chairman of Manufacturers Hanover Trust, and who himself was married to a lady who was a Busch of St. Louis. Flanigan had reservations about his daughter's marriage, and this may have shown a certain prescience because Murray would lose a fair amount of his wife's money when McDonnell & Company crashed. But, the Murray McDonnells would have nine children, and Murray would be something like a grand vizier to Mrs. Onassis, and he would be close to the councils of the church, and perhaps all this would count for something. Sheila McDonnell married Richard Cooley, who lost an arm in the war, but still remained a proficient golf and tennis player, and together they went to San Francisco because, Sheila said, "I want to get away from the clan." Cooley became the president of the Wells Fargo Bank, whereupon he and Sheila were divorced. There were six divorces among Anna and James McDonnell's children, including two by young Gerald McDonnell. As a boy he had suffered from asthma and then he had undergone a mastoid operation. He had spent a part of his childhood sick in bed with a dictionary on his knees, and his father had given him twenty-five cents for each new word he learned. Later, he and a young man from the Grace family thought they might produce plays together, but that never got anywhere, and so Gerald became an academic. He worked toward a doctorate and married a girl named Laura Haggerty. They were divorced, and then Gerald remarried, got divorced, and then remarried the lady he had just divorced. He is now living in New Mexico, where he sees little of the other McDonnells.

Joseph and Theresa Farrell Murray had five daughters, one of whom, a shy, pretty girl, drank too much and died one night in her sleep. Another daughter was divorced and is now in a mental institution. Among the seven children of Jack and Jeanne Murray there were five divorces. Patricia, the first to be married, left Jeffrey Roche and three years later married Sidney B. Wood, who had been a Wimbledon champion and had been ranked ten times among the top ten American players. His son Sidney Wood III died in an automobile accident while he was on a trip with the Yale tennis team, and two years later Deirdre Roche, Patricia Wood's daughter from her first marriage, died in another accident. Patricia Wood asked Father Killeen if he would bury her daughter next to Sidney Wood's son, and Father Killeen refused, saying he would not do that for parents who had been divorced. Patricia and Sidney Wood went to the pastor of the little Polish church, and he did it for them. John, another child of Jack and Jeanne Murray's, was twice divorced. He wrote a novel called *The Devil Walks on Water,* and it was about a rich Irish Catholic family of many members who spent the summers in Southampton.

The family was for the most part pious and even obsessed by the church and her priests, and the hero was a young man in the family who was unlike any of his relatives. Among other things, he was a blasphemer and a successful lecher, and in the first draft of the novel John Murray had the young man die. His agent and his editor, who were not Irish Catholics, thought that was unrealistic and harsh, and asked John Murray to let the young man live. John Murray did, and even allowed his hero to win a lusty glory in Southampton.

Of all the forty-eight grandchildren of Thomas E. Murray, the ones most removed from the traditional Irish Catholic proprieties were the children of Lester and Julia Cuddihy. One became a conscientious objector during World War II and prowled about Southampton in a monk's cowl. Another married his sister's governess, and another, after being thrown out of a great number of schools, was taken to children's court by his mother. Later, when his allowance was cut off, he sued his father for nonsupport. This was Robert Cuddihy, who was thought of as the gayest and most dashing of all the Cuddihys, and whose career, at least in part, inspired John Murray to write *The Devil Walks on Water*. Robert Cuddihy married a Protestant socialite, and after they were divorced he took custody of their five children. He married again, and then nine months later he drove his car into a tree and died. His first wife battled his second wife for the children and won, but then a few years after that she drove her car into a tree and died. The five children were orphans, and Thomas Cuddihy, Robert's brother, brought them into his home. Then, without telling anyone else in the family, he took them to England, put them in school, and left them there. When he returned to New York, Thomas, who had renounced all things Catholic and all things to do with his family as well, was sued for custody of the children by his mother, Julia Cuddihy. However, with the children in England, and with Julia Cuddihy no longer a young woman, there did not seem to be much sense in a long court battle and so the suit was dropped. Thomas had won, and his only point seemed to be that he did not want this generation of Thomas E. Murray's descendants to be raised the same way his own generation had.

Indeed, many of the golden boys and girls paid a price of one kind or another for their privileges, and when some of them renounced what seemed to be a spurious Irish Catholic morality, they paid a price for that, too. A psychiatrist who has treated many wealthy Irish Catholics, including at least a few of Thomas E. Murray's heirs, says that they are forever looking for God, and that when they are faced with freedom they do not know what to do with it.

The children of Thomas E. Murray, Jr., are probably the least venturesome of all the inventor's grandchildren, and they seem to have been the most successful at protecting the old verities and the old Irish Catholic truths. There is even one among them, Bradley, who is a Jesuit priest. It is interesting that there are only two other grandchildren of Thomas E. Murray who went into the church. One is the daughter of Marie Lufkin, who married a Protestant, and the other is a daughter of Jack Murray, who, as all the family knew, was a skeptic. When Jack's daughter Constance said she wanted to become a nun her mother wept and said she would be lost to the world, and Father Keller, remembering that she was only Jack Murray's daughter, said she would never make it. They were both wrong, and when Jeanne, Jack's widow, was dying she had asked Constance what she thought Heaven would be like. Constance, in turn, asked her mother what she thought it would be like. "It means that I'll be with Jack again," Jeanne said. This was twenty-three years after Jack had died, and forty-two years after he and Jeanne had been married. The rest of the family, of course, had been against that marriage all along.

VIII

Barons and Buccaneers

No ONE CAN TELL even remotely how many Irish have graced the pages of the *Social Register,* or become successful in this field or that, because no one can tell even remotely what happened to all the Irish. From the beginning of their time in this country they have been disappearing into the bosoms of families that were neither Irish nor Catholic, and sometimes they have done it without thinking about it, and sometimes they have done it with a certain calculation. "Go West, my friend, and change your name," Dion Boucicault told a young Irishman who complained to him that his wife was being ignored by respectable society. Boucicault had written 124 plays, adapted many more, and acted in things like "The Colleen Bawn," and "The Shaughram." He was a great success at the end of the last century, but being Irish he had a secret sorrow. "I have heard a great deal too much of humiliating slights put upon Irish ladies at balls and there are rules against us at one of the best clubs in town," he wrote. "The Emmetts, I believe, are the one Irish family who have entree everywhere."

Now the Emmetts have not been heard from in generations, and Boucicault himself is a shade, and the young man he counseled may have ended up God knows where. "They melted easily into the westward movements of the 1830's and '40's, shedding their habits from prairie to prairie so that families named O'Donnell, Connor and Delehanty are now discovered drowsing in Protestant pews of Texas and Arkansas," Thomas Beer wrote in 1926. These Irish had lost their faith, but they had kept their names, and that was more than some of the Boston Irish had. Nothing enraged old William Cardinal O'Connell more than the Irish who had fled from both themselves and their church, and he dismissed them as "contemptible toadies who went over body and soul to the enemy and sold their glorious inheritance for a mess of pottage." Some of them, of course, sold out for considerably more than pottage, no matter what the Cardinal said, and their heirs are with us today and doing nicely. As to how they went over, and to which enemy, the Cardinal could not have been more explicit:

> No sooner had they taken their places among the Protestants than they were given places which as Catholics they never could have obtained. And so some of the Murphys became Murfies; some of the O'Briens became Bryants; some of the Delaneys became Delanos. But be it said to the credit of the Catholics of those times, such betrayal and treason were stamped as ignominious and detestable.

Ignominious and detestable, perhaps, but not without purpose, and the Murfies, Bryants, and Delanos were among the first of the closet Irish. Mark Twain found others when he wrote *The Gilded Age,* and he ridiculed some Irish who insisted they were French. Nevertheless, it was never necessary for some of the Irish to skulk about this way because some of the Irish, or partly Irish, had no idea there was any Irish in them at all. Cleveland Amory, for instance, once unearthed a book called *Heredity in Relation to Eugenics,* which was written by a Charles Benedict Davenport in 1911. Davenport said that sometime in the eighteenth century one John Preston of Derry married Elizabeth Patton of Donegal and that together they went to Virginia, where they had five children. From the five children, Davenport said, "have come the most conspicuous of those who bear the names of Preston, Brown, Smith, Carrington, Venable, Payne, Wickliffe, Wooley, Breckenbridge, Benton, Porter and many other names written high in history." These were mostly Virginia and Kentucky aristocrats. Then, Davenport, who may have been a little dotty on the subject, went on to quote "a reliable genealogist," who may even have been a little dottier. The genealogist said:

> They were mostly persons of great talent and thoroughly educated; of large brain and magnificent physique. The men were brave and gallant, the women accomplished and fascinating and incomparably beautiful. There was no aristocracy in America that did not eagerly open its veins for the infusion of Irish blood; and the families of Washington and Randolph and Henry Clay and the Hamptons, Wickliffes, Marshalls, Peytons, Cabells, Crittendens and Ingersolls felt proud of their alliances with this noble Irish family.
>
> They were Governors and Senators and members of Congress, and presidents of colleges and eminent divines, and brave generals, from Virginia, Kentucky, Louisiana, Missouri, California, Ohio, New York, Indiana and South Carolina. There were four Governors of old Virginia. They were members of the Cabinets of Jefferson and Taylor and Buchanan and Lincoln. They had major generals and brigadier generals by the dozen; members of the Senate and House of Representatives by the score; and gallant officers in the Army and Navy by the hundred . . . fifty of them at least the bravest of the brave, sixteen of them dying on the field of battle, and all of them, and more than I can enumerate, children of this one Irish immigrant from the county of Derry, whose relatives are still prominent in that part of Ireland.

The genealogist may have been a fanciful man, although it is pretty to think that some Protestant aristocrats who never cared for the Irish did not know that they themselves were descended from a man from Derry and a woman from Donegal. However, even if they had known it might not have made much difference because no one can be tougher on the Irish than the other Irish. Until her death in 1960, the most powerful social arbiter in America was a woman about whom hardly anything was known except that she was Irish and her name was Bertha Barry.

Mrs. Barry never granted interviews, although for fifty years every publication in America tried to get one, and when *Life* photographers surrounded her home in Florida she dispelled them by calling the police. The cause of all this interest was the *Social Register,* which had been started in 1887 by a man named Louis Keller. He was a peripheral member of society, and among other things he owned a railroad with one locomotive that ran between Summit, Baltusrol, and Newark, New Jersey. His friends called it the "Baltusrol & Pacific."

At some time or another, but presumably before 1900, Keller hired Mrs. Barry, who lived in Summit, and was the daughter of either a railroad conductor or a lineman, and made her his secretary. When Keller died in 1922, Mrs. Barry was entrusted with the editorial, or arbiter, side of the *Register,* and this was at a time when the *Register* was to America approximately what *Burke's Peerage* was to the British Isles. It did no more than list names, addresses, maiden names, children's names, colleges attended, and things like that, but in the absence of anything better it was considered our most reliable guide as to who was in society and who was not. Few people would admit to taking it seriously, although most people did, and in 1925, its greatest year, it put out editions for twenty-five cities. Its correspondents were for the most part poorly paid society reporters and gentlewomen of fallen estate, who clipped the newspapers and recorded births, deaths, marriages, and divorces, and then passed everything on to Mrs. Barry. Early on in her career she was advised by one or two other people as to which candidates for the *Social Register* were worthwhile and which were not, but in time the advisers grew old and died and Mrs. Barry made the judgments by herself. Knowing her place, she never listed her own name in the *Register,* and she hardly ever listed Jews, and over the years she listed very few Irish. Everyone wondered what standards Mrs. Barry was observing, and from time to time someone thought they had guessed. In 1925, just before it dropped their names from its pages forever, the *Social Register* announced the marriage of Leonard Kip Rhinelander to a black lady named Alice Jones. Then, according to Dixon Wecter, Emily Post, the author of *Etiquette,* wrote to Mrs. Barry. "I happen to know," she said, "that you announce all the mésalliances of those on your list; that ends them, and unsuitable behavior ostracizes — a thing which I greatly admire, and one which in certain prominent cases has shown no little courage on your part."

In fact, it took very little courage, and Mrs. Barry was following no standards other than her own. Hidden away in Summit until late in life, when she bought the house in Florida, Mrs. Barry would come into the offices of the *Social Register* once every few weeks, pick up the letters from her correspondents, and then take them home to be pondered. She saw few people and seldom went out, and not even her neighbors knew she had anything to do with the *Register.* She followed her whimsy and Irish morality in all things, and when Alfred Vanderbilt married Jeanne Murray the *Register* announced the marriage and then never mentioned the Vanderbilts again. Their friend John Hay Whitney protested it by saying that the *Register* had long outlived its usefulness and then demanding that henceforth it drop his name, too. Whitney was a man with the most immaculate social credentials and Mrs. Barry ought to have been stricken, but she was not, and so she went on, ignoring the slight, and ignoring Whitney. He, after all, had missed the point. It was not that Alfred Vanderbilt had married for the second time because there were any number of people in the *Social Register* who had done that. It was not that he had married into a family that had neither money nor distinction because the Murrays had some of both. Vanderbilt, however, had married an Irish lady, and Bertha Barry, another one, would not stand for that.

Of course, not all the Irish cared if Mrs. Barry noticed them or not, and some of them were more interested in other things — money and power, for example — and the most successful Irishman in pursuit of both, more so than even Anthony Nicholas Brady, was Thomas Fortune Ryan. Ryan was Irish by descent and Catholic by conversion, and he was the son of a Virginian, who was either a tailor or a farmer. Ryan's earliest history is as lost as that of most Irish patriarchs, but it is established that he was orphaned at fourteen, and that at seventeen he went to Baltimore, where he went to work in the dry goods commission house of John S. Barry. He borrowed money from Barry, and then he married his daugher Ida and took her to New York, where, at the age of twenty-three in 1874, he got his own seat on the Stock Exchange. Ryan was a tall, lanky man with abundant charm, and after he had both made and lost a lot of money, and, according to family legend, been persuaded by Ida Ryan to stay on Wall Street because "it's where you belong," he became associated with Peter A. B. Widener and William Collins Whitney.

This Whitney, the son of a long line of New England intellectuals, had gone to Yale and then to New York, where he became a prominent lawyer. He married Flora Payne, whose brother would become the treasurer of Standard Oil, and he fought hard for virtue in politics, mostly by opposing the Irish rogues in Tammany Hall. Whitney became a distinguished

Secretary of the Navy and a model of great rectitude, and then he became fifty years old and discovered that what he really loved best of all was money. He embraced the Irish rogues, made $40 million off Standard Oil, ordered a gold dinner service from Tiffany, bought the first of two private railroad cars, and then put up stables on Long Island that cost $2 million. Whitney, Henry Adams wrote, "had thrown away the usual objects of political ambition like the ashes of smoked cigarettes; he had turned to other amusements, satiated every taste, gorged every appetite, won every object that New York afforded, and not yet satisfied, had carried his field of activity abroad until New York no longer knew what most to envy, his horses or his houses."

Whitney was Ryan's closest associate, and the other one, Peter A. B. Widener, while not as magnificent, was no pauper, either. He had been a butcher's boy in Philadelphia, who went on to own a meat market, and then to spend a good deal of time drinking beer and playing poker with local politicians. In 1873, he became the city treasurer of Philadelphia, and, what with one thing or another, and in partnership with William B. Elkins, soon was running the Philadelphia streetcar system. This was about the time that Anthony Nicholas Brady, having already hired Thomas E. Murray in Albany, was moving into New York. Brady joined with Ryan, Whitney, and Widener, and together they took over New York's rapid-transit operations. Ryan and Whitney took over more than the others, however, and Ryan began to grow seriously rich. He moved into railroads, streetlighting companies, and coal mines, and then he put together a group of financiers who took over the National Cigarette Company. He merged that with the Union Tobacco Company, which he and Brady, Whitney, and Widener already controlled, and then he fought James Duke for what was left of the tobacco industry. King Leopold of Belgium asked Ryan to straighten out the tangled

affairs of his diamond mines in the Congo, which he did, and
then he battled J. P. Morgan, and lost, for control of the
Equitable Life Insurance Company. Whitney said that Ryan
was "the most adroit, suave and noiseless man that American
finance has ever known," and Bernard Baruch said he was
"the most resourceful man I ever knew intimately on Wall
Street." Others said he was a cold buccaneer, with a heart of
stone. J. P. Morgan, however, just said he was "an Irish
upstart."

Whitney died in 1904, and a short while after that a grand
jury looked into New York's rapid-transit system and con-
cluded that it was a mess. The Metropolitan Street Railway
Company had been virtually looted, and Ryan, the grand jury
said, had done things that were "dishonest and probably crimi-
nal." Ryan never really denied it, although he did hire a press
agent called Quigg, who was supposed to see that henceforth
only nice things were said about him. Ryan also paid $10,000
to "Colonel" William D'Alton Mann, a fraudulent old black-
mailer who published a scandal sheet called *Town Topics,* and
who, until he was brought to court, would tap the rich for
money in return for the promise that *Town Topics* would say
nothing mean about them. In this, at least, Ryan was in good
company because even J. P. Morgan gave the Colonel $2500,
although the Colonel seems to have made his biggest score off
James R. Keene, who gave him $90,000. Ryan was beginning
to live fairly magnificently by now. When the grand jury
looked at him he was worth about $50 million, and a few
years later he was worth twice that. He put up a five-story
graystone mansion on Fifth Avenue with a huge conservatory
and garden, and filled it with statues and busts, three of them
by Rodin, and many of them of himself. Moreover, Ida Barry
Ryan wanted space for her roses, and so to please her Ryan
bought the adjoining mansion. It had belonged to Charles T.
Yerkes, who had put several million dollars into it, but Ryan

pulled it down, anyway. He left standing only the circular marble staircase, nothing more, and on it Mrs. Ryan entwined her roses. Presumably, this made her happy, although it didn't do much for the marriage, which had been declining for years. Ida Barry Ryan was a devout Catholic, more devout than her husband, and in 1907 Pope Pius X made her a Countess of the Holy Roman Empire. She was famous for her good works and piety, and she turned whole rooms of the mansion into a sacristy. This frequently made her husband look elsewhere for amusement, although in the great tradition of Irish Catholic *grandes dames* she got him to give $20 million to the church. Ida Ryan died in 1917, and twelve days after she died, Ryan, at the age of sixty-six, married again. His new bride, Mary T. Nicoll, a lady from an old and prominent New York family, had been married twice before, and Ryan's sons were displeased. Allan, the oldest, said the marriage was "disrespectful, disgraceful and indecent," and Thomas Fortune Ryan remembered what he said. When Ryan died in 1928, leaving an estate of $135 million, Allan's share of it was two shirt studs.

The Ryans may not be the most prominent Irish Catholic family of our time, although if for no other reasons than the money and the miseries that were visited on them, they may be the most spectacular. Thomas Fortune Ryan had five sons — Allan, John Barry, Clendenin, William Kane, and Joseph. William Kane and Joseph died before their father did, and when Joseph died he left his wife only $100. The rest of his estate went to an actress. Years later, Joseph's only son, who owned the Mont Tremblant ski lodge, was an apparent suicide. Allan Ryan, the son to whom Thomas Fortune Ryan left the shirt studs, had in a happier day been given his father's old seat on the Stock Exchange, and had used it to become one of the great bulls of Wall Street. By 1916, he had gotten the controlling interest in the Stutz Motor Car Company and had made himself its president. He had also aroused the dislike of the genteel Protestant cutthroats who made up the Wall Street establishment, and after a great battle with them over the Stutz stock, Allan Ryan filed a petition for bankruptcy. His debts, he said, were $32,435,477, which included $60.36 he owed to the Buckley School for tuition, $13.75 to the Montauk Club for dues, and $768.68 to Charles & Company for groceries. His assets, he said, were $643,533. The same year that he filed the bankruptcy petition, Allan Ryan had a court battle with George Maxwell, the president of the American Society of Composers, Authors and Publishers, over the affections of Maxwell's wife. Three years later, Ryan himself was divorced and he married a woman named Irene McKenna. Then, in 1933, he was sued for $100,000 by his maid, on whom, she said, he had forced his affections. Allan Ryan died in 1940.

John Barry Ryan, the second of Thomas Fortune Ryan's sons, wrote poetry under the name of Barrie Vail, and married a girl called Nan Morgan, with whom he had ten children. He was the most whimsical of the Ryans, and perhaps because he was, he stayed out of serious trouble. When a friend or relative got married, John Barry Ryan always gave the same gift — twenty-four letter openers. Mostly, however, he was known for his vagaries about money. At the Saratoga horse sales one August, he bought a colt from Mrs. Payne Whitney, and in the way of rich people who know another well enough he did not immediately pay her. A few months later, he visited Mrs. Whitney at Hot Springs, Arkansas, and with great grace and assurance said he was temporarily short of cash, and asked if she would mind waiting for payment of the debt, which, after all, was only a few thousand dollars. With equal grace and assurance, Mrs. Whitney said she would not mind waiting at all, although presumably she wondered what had happened to John Barry Ryan's money. Then Ryan left, and returned to

New York. He did not return just any old way, however; he chartered an entire private train from the Chesapeake & Ohio. Unlike his father and brothers, John Barry Ryan never showed much interest in business, and was far more consumed by his poetry. The magazine editors to whom he sent the poetry, though, were ordinarily not impressed, and Ryan once commissioned a vanity publisher in Boston to put out a volume for distribution to his friends. When the books were ready, Ryan, disdaining any usual way of getting them to New York, hired a pilot to fly to Boston, pick up the books, and bring them back. Yet John Barry Ryan could, if he wanted to, pursue small economies, and once he was discovered on one of the fairways of the Piping Rock Club, heating a can of Campbell's tomato soup over a small fire. It was, he said, his lunch.

Clendenin, the last remaining son of Thomas Fortune Ryan, worked on Wall Street, married well, and had four children. There was not much to distinguish him one way or the other, or so it seemed, and in 1923 he was sued by a showgirl for "room rent," which was the kind of thing that was always happening to the Ryans. Still, there was a darkness and guilt to these Irish Catholic Ryans, and in 1939, in the library of the home that Thomas Fortune Ryan had owned, Clendenin put his head into a gas fireplace and killed himself. Eighteen years later, in the same house, his son Clendenin Jr. committed suicide, too. Just before his death he had promised to pay for the famous Rose Window in St. Patrick's Cathedral. His widow did it for him.

That was the generation that followed the patriarch Thomas Fortune Ryan. The children born to that generation, the grandchildren of Thomas Fortune Ryan, were further removed than their parents from the money and publicity that was attendant on their grandfather and his wife, the Papal Countess, and perhaps because they were they seemed to suffer fewer disasters. There were divorces and remarriages among them, almost too many to count, but some of the careers were successful, and some of the marriages worked, and were even interesting. Nina, a daughter of John Barry Ryan, for example, married Philip Carroll, a direct descendant of Charles Carroll of Carrollton, the old Catholic grandee. Her brother John Barry Ryan, Jr., married Margaret Kahn, the daughter of the famous Otto Kahn. Kahn, the German Jewish financier, who through his patronage once virtually saved the Metropolitan Opera House from expiring, had a house on Long Island that looked like a Norman castle and at one time had a staff of 125 people running it. Margaret Kahn and John Barry Ryan, Jr., had two children, Virginia, who married Lord David Ogilvy, and John Barry Ryan III, who married Dorinda Dixon. John and Dorinda, or D.D., seem to be the most exposed of all their generation of Ryans, and they are seen frequently in that small stylish world of New York celebrities who move along the East Side in the winter and Nantucket or the Hamptons in the summer. There seems to be nothing that would connect them to the old sacristy on Fifth Avenue at all.

It is patently clear that the Irish rich seldom seemed to have an easy time of it, and sometimes Irish who only married into the rich had a hard time of it, too. In 1900, for instance, Nora McMullen married Andrew Mellon. She was the beautiful granddaughter of Peter Guinness, the Dublin brewer, and he was the Pittsburgh banker with cold eyes and tight lips who was building a great fortune. She was twenty and he was forty-five, and the marriage lasted just long enough to produce two children, Ailsa, who until her death was Mrs. David Bruce, and Paul, who is the sportsman and patron of the arts. In her divorce statement, Nora McMullen Mellon said this about Pittsburgh and her husband: "The whole community was as cold and hard as the steel it made, and chilled the heart to the core . . . Nights that I spent in my baby boy's bedroom, nursing these thoughts of his future, my husband, locked in his study, nursed his dollars, millions of dollars, maddening dollars, nursed larger and bigger at the cost of priceless sleep, irretrievable health and happiness." It is possible that Mrs. Mellon was only feeling sorry for herself, and that it was simply a bad match from the beginning. She soon went back to Dublin with a handsome settlement, visiting rights to the children, and an abiding dislike for Pittsburgh.

Mrs. Mellon did not know it, but for the Irish, Boston was much worse. One could be Irish and still get rich in Pittsburgh, or, for that matter, in Akron, Detroit, or Cleveland, but in Boston that was almost out of the question except for politicians. By 1900, Boston had atrophied and gone stale, and the grandsons of the daring old Yankees who had built the city were clipping coupons and losing themselves in their genealogies. "Much that was only vulgar — inertia, ignorance, economic despotism — masqueraded as high-minded New England conservatism," William Shannon wrote, and what was proportionately the most Irish city in America became a graveyard for the energetic and adventurous. Some of the energetic and adventurous Irish, Joseph P. Kennedy, for one, left to find their lives elsewhere, while the ones who stayed behind joined the civil service, or turned into sour and boozy men with shards instead of hope in their hearts. By 1940, Shannon found, only four of the thirty directors of the Boston Chamber of Commerce were Irish, and no big department store and only one small bank had been run by the Irish. The New England Council, which was supposed to lead the economic recovery of the area, and which had been founded in 1925, did not have a single Irishman as an officer, a committee chairman, or a member of its executive committee until sometime after World War II. In terms of wealth, at least, the only Irish businessmen who stayed Irish and Catholic and still seemed to make it were the ones who got to Boston before the blight set in.

John Cavanagh arrived in 1821 after selling his shoe-making business in Dublin the year before, and set about making fine shoes once again. His son James went into the business with him and invented machines that made heels and soles. That was the beginning of the United Shoe Machinery Corporation, which in time grew so large that it had to hire Louis Brandeis to defend it against antitrust laws. It also made James Cavanagh a millionaire at the age of thirty, with enough distinction to be asked to run for the Senate. He declined, just as years later he declined the papal honors that were offered to him. "I will accept," he said, "when it is seen fit to extend them not just to the wealthy, but to someone like a violinist, or a mother who has successfully raised ten children." James Cavanagh, who had ten children himself, was obviously something more than just a businessman, and for amusement he bred hogs that had no cleft in their hooves and crossed country gentleman and yellow bantam corn. Finally, however, old Boston's shabbiness toward the Irish Catholics became too much even for him, and so in 1890, at the age of fifty-nine, he bought a home on Clinton Avenue in Brooklyn. He took a box at the opera, became a friend of J. P. Morgan's, and bought a yacht on which he kept a cow so that his grandchildren could have fresh milk. One of the grandchildren, Edward Cavanagh, became the Deputy Mayor of New York under Robert Wagner. Edward's sister, Barbara, became Wagner's second wife. Grandfather Cavanagh died in 1909, leaving behind him a great deal of money, a distaste for Boston, and a widow who had shared both his life and his distaste. She soon went to Paris, where she died in 1947 at the age of 104.

Cavanagh was not a spectacular Irishman, only a graceful one, and lacking an appetite for either riotous living or great feats of daring he was largely unheard of in his time. On the other hand, everyone knew his contemporary, Diamond Jim Brady, who had been born of poor Irish parents on the Lower

West Side of New York and gone on to become the most celebrated glutton and wastrel of his time. Brady was not an entirely foolish man, however, and much of his roistering was really an advertisement for himself. He was a railroad man who had been chief clerk to the general manager of the Vanderbilts' New York Central & Hudson River Railroad, and he carried around with him a great knowledge of railroading. When someone developed a handsaw that could cut rails as they were laid, rather than having them cut at a foundry and then sent over great distances, Brady left the New York Central to sell it. Then he began to sell other kinds of railroad equipment, and because his commissions were extraordinarily high he became rich. Everyone wanted to do business with a man whose diamond studs, cuff links, rings, tie pins, and buttons were supposed to be worth $2 million, and who, for amusement, gave his friends gold-plated bicycles. The one he gave Lillian Russell cost $10,000 and was alleged to have diamond chips, emeralds, rubies, and sapphires mounted on the spokes of the wheels. Miss Russell, wearing a white serge suit, would mount it very carefully on Sundays and appear in Central Park for the photographers.

Besides this kind of largess, Brady was known for his compulsive eating. According to Lucius Beebe, Brady would eat not only the twelve-course dinners that were found in the better restaurants in the early part of this century, he would have three or four helpings of the things he really liked. He would begin with a gallon of chilled orange juice, and then go on to something like six-dozen lynnhaven oysters, a saddle of mutton, venison chops, a roasting chicken, a brace of ducks, partridges or pheasants, and a twelve-egg soufflé. Watching him eat, Beebe wrote, "was a spectacle that unnerved some spectators, while others gathered around . . . to cheer him on his progress through the cutlets and make side bets on whether or not he'd fall dead before dessert."

Brady left nothing behind him when he died other than a legendary vulgarity, although another Irishman who was born in New York left a dynasty. This was the celebrated Captain Richard King, whose impoverished parents apprenticed him to a jeweler when he was nine years old. Two years later, he stowed away on a ship bound for Mobile, and within a few years after that was the captain of a riverboat himself. He fought in the Mexican and Seminole wars, became a friend of Robert E. Lee's, and began buying land in Texas. This was the beginning of the King Ranch, and when Captain King died in 1885 at the age of sixty-one, he left behind a place of 500,000 acres, with 100,000 cattle, 20,000 sheep, 10,000 horses, and 1000 people on it. It survives today, far larger, and it is still run by his heirs.

There were other Irish conquistadors, of course, not so wealthy as Ryan, so boisterous as Diamond Jim, or so culti- vated as Cavanagh, perhaps, but they came along, enriching the Irish American culture, and detracting from it, too. For one, there was Edward L. Doheny, the oil man. He was born to poor Irish immigrants in Fond du Lac, Wisconsin, and he was blessed with daring, venality, and uncommon good luck, the best evidence of which was that he never went to jail for bribing Secretary of the Interior Albert Fall in the Teapot Dome scandal. Doheny, unlike the other patriarchs, was deeply interested in Ireland and gave money to something called the Irish Freedom Movement. His wife was more inter- ested in the church, and she got Doheny to give vast sums, some of which built St. Vincent's Cathedral in Los Angeles. There are young Dohenys in Los Angeles today unaware of any of it.

Another conquistador was Tom Walsh of Clonmel in County Tipperary. He came to America in 1869, drifted west, struck silver first and then gold, and finally settled down in Washington, D.C., where he and his family lived a baronial

life on Massachusetts Avenue. Tom Walsh bought and
flaunted just about everything, and when his daughter, Evalyn, was ten he got her a blue Victoria coach, with a pair of
matched sorrels to pull it and a coachman in silk hat and
gloves to drive it. It was the first of a long series of expensive
acquisitions for Evalyn, and when she grew up and married
Edward Beale McLean, the son of the publisher of the Washington *Post,* she and her husband tried hard to establish a
record for general profligacy and lavish living. McLean's best-
known stunt was to pee in the fireplace of the East Room of
the White House one night, while his wife became famous
chiefly as the owner of the Hope Diamond. It was supposed to
carry a curse, and Evalyn Walsh McLean, reverting to some
Tipperary impulse, got a Monsignor Walsh to exorcise it. The
legend is that when he did a great clap of thunder smote the
skies and a mighty wind rushed up from out of nowhere. It
hardly mattered. Edward Beale McLean still became an alcoholic, and finally he left Evalyn to pursue Marion Davies'
sister in Europe. Poor Evalyn became a famous Washington
hostess, and an alcoholic and morphine addict as well. Her
son was run over by an automobile, and her daughter died
from an overdose of sleeping pills. Evalyn was sad all her life;
many of the Irish heirs to money are.

IX

Rites of Passage

THOSE WHO WERE THERE remember it as very grand indeed, and *Life* magazine said that it probably would "begin a new party-giving era in U.S. history." The party, *Life* said, "ranks with the costliest balls of Newport at its grandest," and while this was true because it cost something like $250,000, it really did not begin a new era so much as it ended an old one. Charlotte Ford, a great-granddaugher of Thomas E. Murray, was its most prominent survivor, and when her parents gave her the party they did it with a flourish. "I guess they'll know who we are now," Charlotte's mother, Anna, had written when she married Henry Ford nineteen years before, and now every-one would know who her daughter was, too. Her debut was like the coming out of royalty, which, in this egalitarian coun-try, was truly what it was, and until the Kennedys burst on us the next year with their assortment of princes and princesses, Charlotte Ford, at the age of seventeen, was the natural and foremost heir to all good things that were both Irish and Catholic. The world having changed by then, no one quite thought of it that way, but Charlotte had the Murrays and McDonnells on one side of the family, and the Fords, al-though their Irish connection had long since been forgotten, on the other, and she had been raised with every propriety. She was the last of the golden boys and girls, and when she walked gracefully through the hallway that led into the reception room of the country club at Grosse Pointe Farms on the night of December 21, 1959, she walked through 2 million magnolia leaves that had been flown up from Mississippi the day before. The idea was to make the country club look like a French chateau out of the eighteenth century, and although the magnolia leaves were only whimsy, they showed that the Fords were determined to do things grandly. Certainly they were determined to spend money, and they did it loudly. Besides the magnolia leaves, there were hedges, blooming trees, tapestries, a fountain, and scattered all about the five rooms of the country club $60,000 worth of flowers. Charlotte's debut had taken a year to plan, and the twenty-seven young men who were there as ushers even had medallions hung around their necks with her initials on them. There were Du Ponts, Firestones, Roosevelts, Mr. and Mrs. Gary Cooper, a Churchill, and the editor of *Vogue* among the 1100 guests, and on the night before the debut Charlotte's uncles and aunts on the Ford side had given her a dinner party. Charlotte's nubility was being announced with style, and that night at the country club Henry Ford had begun by dancing with her, and then he had leaped and capered about, and finally jumped up on the bandstand and led Meyer Davis' orchestra in "Hey-Ba-Ba-Re-Bop." Anne McDonnell Ford, a child of propriety, frowned.

Charlotte Ford, by everyone's account, was a perfectly pleasant young woman, and in a white satin gown embroidered with pink flowers, tourmalines, and pearls, she sat on the floor of the library surrounded by friends, all of them as virginal looking as she, and listened to Nat King Cole sing. He had been summoned at her request, and he had sung of unrequited yearnings and youthful passions. So far, Charlotte had never had very much to do with any of that, and except for a year at finishing school in Florence, and a year long before that at the Grosse Pointe University School, she and her sister, Anne, had been largely in the care and keeping of the nuns of the Order of the Sacred Heart. Long afterward, Charlotte said that that part of her life had been like prison. Anne said, "I don't know how we stood it. I think we thought it was that way for everyone." It was not, of course, and neither were the other things that made up their lives. As small girls, they were once taken at Christmas to the Dearborn estate of their great-grandfather Henry Ford, and on the estate was a playhouse with a Santa Claus inside. "Help yourself to whatever you want," Santa had said. The toys were stacked up to the ceiling.

Besides Dearborn, Grosse Pointe Farms, and the convents, Charlotte and Anne Ford quite naturally grew up in Southampton. Their mother, being a McDonnell, would spend the summers nowhere else than in that protectorate, and so Charlotte and Anne and a multiplicity of first cousins became the fourth generation of Murrays and McDonnells to go through rites of passage in the Irish Catholic compound. Few of them, however, were ever told about old Tom, their great-grandfather, although he had made Southampton possible for all of them, but his daughter Anna McDonnell and his son Thomas E. Murray, Jr., still towered over the compound, visible reminders of the faith incarnate. Every Sunday morning after Mass in the private chapel, Anna McDonnell would gather her grandchildren together for a breakfast of pancakes and bacon. This, they remembered later, was pleasant. By the 1950s, however, the verities were beginning to change and old things were passing almost unnoticed. Cardinal Spellman was still occupying the chancery and Pope Pius the Vatican, but socially the Irish Catholics were in the ascendancy. The year before Charlotte Ford made her debut, for example, *Life* had gathered together what it called the "Young Leaders of New York Society," and photographed them, beautifully gowned and jeweled, for a cover. Among the young leaders was Charlotte Harris, one of Anna and James McDonnell's children, and another was Cathie di Montzemolo, a daughter of Jack and Jeanne Murray's. Near them was Gloria Schiff, whose name had been O'Connor, and in back of her was Anita Colby, who was probably the most quintessential Irish Catholic of them all.

In the late 1930s, Miss Colby, a young woman of extraordinary beauty and determination, had become America's first great model, appearing on so many magazine covers that she became known as "The Face." Ultimately, she went to Hollywood, where she appeared in ten movies, generally just walking on and off without saying much, but doing it with such style that it usually was nice to see her, nonetheless. Then she became a movie publicist for David O. Selznick, who made her Feminine Director of his studio. She was put in charge not only of the good looks, but more importantly for a lady of her persuasions, the manners and morals of Mr. Selznick's stars. This so interested *Time* magazine that it put her back on a cover again; the week before it had used General Eisenhower, who had just won the war in Europe. Later, Miss Colby, who had been born Anita Counihan, the daughter of Daniel Counihan who drew the "Betty Boop" and "Little Napoleon" cartoons, and whose great-uncle had been in the first Irish Parliament, became a columnist, the owner of a news syndicate, and the author of a widely read beauty book. The beauty book said things in it like "be a good girl," and "take a walk, walk to church," for above all Anita Colby was a child of the church, its pieties locked in her heart. She traveled for the church and spoke for it, and over the years she kept up a partnershp with the clergy that other Irish ladies could only admire. Miss Colby spoke at communion breakfasts and sodality dinners, testified for the Christophers, Opus Dei, and virtually any other Catholic group that asked her to, and in return, she sometimes said, had been given what seemed to be the world's largest collection of rosaries blessed by the Pope. "Can't you ever get anyone else for the road show?" Miss Colby would say to Cardinal Spellman, and she would speak with the mock asperity that only ladies who were close to him were privileged to use. She would mean that if he were not after Rosalind Russell, or Loretta Young, or Captain Eddie Rickenbacker to go out and appear on a dais somewhere or other, then he was after her. ("I like Loretta Young so much," Miss Colby said with great approval not long ago. "Do you know that when she goes out with a man on a date she always insists that another couple go with them for appearance sake?" Miss Young was then in her sixties.)

Anita Colby had beauty and charm, and as the years went by and she continued to live with her parents, she had her maidenhood, too. Sometimes this seemed to endear her to the clergy most of all. Then, in 1970, at the age of fifty-three, she chose to marry an executive of the J. P. Stevens Textile Company, and although her friends applauded, the clergy wept. They had, they said, been betrayed, and Miss Colby felt badly herself. Palen Flagler, the man Miss Colby chose, had been married years before, and then only briefly, but he had been divorced, and that was against the rules of the game. Miss Colby could not be married in the eyes of the church, or at least in that part of the church to which she subscribed, and all her good works were going for nothing. She fought, she wept, she screamed, and the clergy divided themselves, some saying that if you made an exception for her then you had to make an exception for everyone, and others saying that this was "our Anita," and so for God's sake let's be sensible. One bishop who had promised to intercede for her at Rome never did so, and even worked against her. Finally, however, Miss Colby just said the hell with it, and decided that she would marry Mr. Flagler, anyway. Deep in the catacombs or wherever it is that books on canon law are stored, a scholar then discovered something called the St. Paul privilege. It meant that despite the groom's earlier marriage, he and Miss Colby could still be safely wed. They were, and Terence Cardinal Cooke quietly sent them his blessing.

These were deadly serious matters, legalities touching on the soul, and Charlotte and Anne Ford, although younger than Miss Colby, had them in their bloodstreams, where they had been implanted by family tradition and all that the nuns of the Sacred Heart held dear. Until quite recently, the daughters of the pious Irish rich simply had to go to a Sacred Heart convent, while the sons went to either Portsmouth Priory or Canterbury. Canterbury was established in 1915 in New Milford, Connecticut, to give boys "a sound college preparation, as offered by the best nonsectarian boarding schools, together with thorough training in the doctrines and practices of the Catholic church." In other words, it was the Irish answer to Groton, St. Paul's, and Exeter. Portsmouth Priory was founded in Portsmouth, Rhode Island, in 1926 by the Reverend J. Hugh Diman. Father Diman had been a celibate Episcopalian priest, earnestly solicitous of the sons of the rich Episcopalians who visited Newport, and for them he had founded Diman's School for Small Boys, which later became St. George's. Then, at the age of sixty-three, Father Diman embraced Catholicism, entering a Benedictine monastery in Scotland and starting out on a journey of the soul, which, in a way, turned out to be not much of a journey after all. Wisely, the Benedictines sent him back to America to do what he did best, and so he established Portsmouth Priory and almost immediately made it into an even more fashionable school for Irish Catholic boys than Canterbury. For one thing, Father Diman had been an Episcopalian, and the Irish admired Episcopalian manners. For another, Father Diman was an ascetic. They admired that, too.

For girls, however, there was only a Sacred Heart convent. A generation of Murray and McDonnell girls went to the one

at 54th Street and Madison Avenue. Later it was moved to
Otto H. Kahn's old Italian Renaissance mansion at 91st Street
and Fifth Avenue, where, inevitably, it became known as the
Kahn-vent. Nonetheless, it still retained all its graces and
hunger for decorum, and even the nuns who taught there were
for the most part gently bred ladies from Irish families themselves. A Murray who attended Georgetown as a young man
in the late 1950s remembers once being summoned to the
convent along with a number of other Irish Catholic eligibles
for a dance. He says they went by bus, and that as each young
man stepped off the bus he was met by an elderly nun, who
looked down at his ankles. She was looking to see if anyone
was wearing sweat socks. Fortunately, the young Murray
gentleman was not; he was wearing suitable black ones. He
says he does not recall now what the penalty was for wearing
sweat socks, but that he assumes it must have been something
terrible.

Anne and Charlotte Ford were admitted to the world of the
Sacred Heart at kindergarten in Grosse Pointe. They remained there through the seventh grade, and then they were
taken out and sent to the Grosse Pointe University School for
a year. When that year was up they went to the Sacred Heart
convent in Noroton, Connecticut, where their mother and her
sisters had gone before them, and where, their mother said,
she liked the atmosphere. "It was very, very strict," Anne
Ford said years later, when she was Mrs. Giancarlo Uzielli.
"You weren't allowed to be yourself. A lot of girls started
out in the ninth grade, but couldn't take it and so they'd drop
out. We couldn't leave, couldn't go home. My mother and
father wouldn't let us. I said I wanted to leave, but they
wouldn't listen. I cried every time I got on the train to go
back."

Noroton taught a girl to be a lady, full of grace, skilled in
the small arts of giving a really correct dinner party, and

knowledgeable about picking out the proper linens. These things were not so much taught as they were learned by osmosis; they were in the air. A Sacred Heart girl also knew how to sit, how to stand, and how never to cross her legs at the knees, only at the ankles. There is nothing wrong in knowing these things, and indeed there are old Sacred Heart girls about today who are models of charm and taste. There are others who wear the mark of Goody Two Shoes on them, but that is something else again. The real problem was in the other things that went with a Sacred Heart education, particularly at Noroton. Within them were seeds that had been planted at the Maynooth Seminary outside Dublin by French Jansenists 200 years before, and had been nettlesome to the Irish ever since. Mostly, they had to do with sex. Sex scared Noroton half to death. Procreation was one thing, and the Sacred Heart girl was told that her "role is central to the design of creation," but this had to do with motherhood. Sex was different It was embarrassing; worse, it was improper, and one can never underestimate the way the American Irish shunned anything improper.

All the girls at Noroton when Anne and Charlotte were there were Irish, with the exception of one girl, a Bourbon, who qualified because of her illustrious family, and a few Cuban girls. Rich Cuban society in the time before Fidel Castro was a colonial society, and it was a good deal like that of the French, startingly proper and suffused with good manners. Therefore, the Cuban girls qualified, too. All the girls, Irish, Cuban, and the solitary Bourbon, had their letters slit open and read before they reached them. Letters from parents were permissible; a letter from a boy, even a letter with the most innocent message, would never reach anyone. Possibly it was exorcised. The Sacred Heart girls were allowed no phone calls, no radio, no television, no magazines, and, until the twelfth grade, no newspapers. Then they were allowed to read the *New York Times,* which, in those days at least, had a reputation for never corrupting anyone. The girls at Noroton also walked to class in single file and in perfect silence, and indeed solitude and silence sometimes seemed to be the things most prized of all.

There was Mass every morning at 6:30, and then benediction every afternoon at 5:00. At 10:15 every morning a bell rang, and the girls would get fruit juice. The good thing about this was that they could talk to one another while they drank it. Then, at 10:30, another bell rang. The juice was finished, and so was the talking. Silence again. On most afternoons, however, there were sports, and the girls, swaddled to the knees in their pale blue gym bloomers, could talk to one another again. Mostly, they were expected to talk about basketball or field hockey, and when sports were over there was silence again. Close friendships among the girls were not encouraged, and in truth they were actively discouraged. The nuns worried about everything, and God only knew what young girls might do if they were thrown together in the first flushes of pubescence. In Anne Ford's first year at Noroton, the girls were allowed to take only three showers a week. In her second year they were allowed to take five. These they took alone, too. For some reason all the convent's own, the Noroton girls were not allowed to keep any books in their rooms, and so they did all their studying in a great communal hall. Possibly it was easier to see what they were up to that way. At 9:00 P.M., a bell rang, and the girls were sent to their rooms. Alone and in silence then, they got ready for bed. At 9:15 another bell rang. The day was over, the lights went out, and God help any child who was found in another's room.

It was really not much of a life to prepare anyone for the world, leaving the girls with mingled feelings of guilt, anger, frustration, and rebellion, but the Reverend Mother explained it this way: "She who can bear the small trials of daily discipline will not falter at those crises in life which require firmness and solitude." Perhaps, but perhaps it was just the old Irish habit of confusing flagellation and respectability. Everytime a Sacred Heart girl at Noroton passed the Reverend Mother, who was a gently bred Coakely lady from Youngstown, Ohio, she had to curtsy. The girls wore plaid dresses in the morning and gray flannel in the afternoon, and there was a test for whether the dresses were long enough. The girls had to kneel on the floor, and if their knees showed when they did this the dresses were too short. Impropriety was everywhere.

When Charlotte Ford was finished at Noroton, she went to the Lefleuron School in Florence. Anne, a year behind her, waited and then she went to Briarcliff. The nuns disliked both places, and they thought it would have been infinitely better for the girls if they had gone on to Manhattanville College of the Sacred Heart in Purchase, New York. Manhattanville, in fact, seemed to be the only college that the nuns at Noroton recognized. If pressed, the nuns would send their girls' records on to other Catholic colleges, but only after they had argued for Manhattanville first. Moreover, the nuns had a policy of simply refusing to send school records on to any non-Catholic school at all, and when Anne Ford was released from the convent she had to gather up her own records and pass them on to Briarcliff herself. All of this was in 1960, when ecumenism, Vatican II, and a Catholic President were waiting, perhaps not to change the world, but certainly to change it a little. The old order was passing, but for the Irish rich it existed in its last days in places like Portsmouth Priory and the convents of the Order of the Sacred Heart.

In years to come, Charlotte Ford would not be exactly sure when she first met Stavros Niarchos, although she would think it was the summer of either 1959 or 1960, when she and Anne were in St. Tropez and Niarchos was anchored off Antibes in his *Creole,* the largest private yacht in the world. Charlotte, however, could recall that she was introduced to Niarchos by George Livanos, who was something of a beau, and, coincidentally, the brother of Niarchos' third wife. Livanos drove Charlotte and Anne over to Antibes, and Niarchos suggested that they all spend the night on the *Creole.* Charlotte refused, saying that she didn't have the proper clothes, and years later saying that she had thought that Niarchos was just another "dirty old man." Niarchos was then fifty, and leaving aside the question of whether he was a dirty old man or not, he was unquestionably an original, matched in his tastes and habits only by the other members of that strange, familial tribe, the rich Greek shipowners. To a man, they are tough and astute, and they do not care whether a fascisti colonel or a leftist republican runs the government in Athens because they can do business with either one. Entrenched in their wealth, yachts, private islands, and homes all over the world, they are the figments of a capomafioso's dream. Furthermore, in the matriarchal land of Greece they are inordinately proud of their sexual capacities, and among themselves they recognize only two kinds of marriages. The first kind is arranged, as when Aristotle Onassis, for example, took Tina Livanos as his bride, and it has less to do with the heart than it does with whose ships get to fly Liberian flags of convenience. The other kind of marriage is possibly even romantic. The Greek shipowners are enchanted by naive women, and about them they establish a protectorate, which is made up of their yachts and private islands, and their sense of machismo, too. They wear these women like ornaments, and while it may be hard on first considering it to think of Jacqueline Onassis as being naive, it is even harder to think of her as being any other way. The matching up of Charlotte Ford and Stavros Niarchos was ordained and inexorable, wealth being attracted to wealth, which is what wealth almost always is attracted to, and a Sacred Heart innocence enthralling and being enthralled by a shipowner's machismo. Besides, there was a natural progression in the history of the McDonnells. Charlotte's mother had married Henry Ford and added luster to her name, giving herself a touch of recognition that otherwise she would not have had. With Stavros Niarchos, her daughter was stepping up, too.

After that first meeting on the *Creole*, Charlotte Ford and Stavros Niarchos did not see one another again for five years. Charlotte and Anne, meanwhile, were regularly gracing the society pages and frequently turning up on everyone's best-dressed list, where Charlotte said she favored things by Dior and Courrèges. Often, Charlotte also submitted herself to newspaper interviews, and in one of them, in the *Journal-American* in 1965, she was asked about marriage.

"I have no ideal man," she said. "I'm just waiting for the right one to come along. If he were poor and I loved him, of course I'd marry him."

Of course, and by 1965, Anne McDonnell Ford, who was by then divorced from Henry, had fled Detroit forever and was living in a duplex on Park Avenue, a few doors away from her mother, Anna McDonnell. Charlotte and Anne were also living in the duplex, and it was a place with high ceilings, ornate chandeliers, décor by McMillen, and a long hallway with the bedrooms of all three Ford ladies coming off it. A hairdresser came by frequently to minister to them, and when he was asked what the apartment was like he said he really didn't know, but that "it was sort of like going down a bowling alley at night." The three Ford ladies, mother and daughters, were getting as much publicity on the society pages in the 1960s as the Cushing girls of Boston did in the 1930s. The Cushing girls, however, were not Irish and the Ford ladies were, and generally speaking these things cause more problems for the Irish.

In 1965, Charlotte met Niarchos again, this time in St. Moritz. Charlotte was with Harry Platt, who would later be the president of Tiffany, and together they were invited to Niarchos' house for a party. It was in honor of Christina Ford, who had just married Henry, and Charlotte and Christina, who sat together and talked for the first time, hit it off famously. When the party was over, Christina turned to Charlotte and said, "Did you notice how Stavros was looking at you?" It was the beginning of something, its dimensions yet unexplored, but obviously a long way from the convent. The day after the party, Niarchos arranged a skiing outing with Charlotte and a few friends, and the rest is almost history. That summer, the Ford ladies chartered the *Shemara,* a 212-foot yacht that was owned by Lady Dockery and nicely fitted out with gold bathroom fixtures. Charlotte's mother was aboard with her new beau, Teddy Basset, a convivial man whose deep interests were gin rummy and backgammon, and who later married a millionaire's daughter from Palm Beach. The *Shemara* cruised the Mediterranean for a month, and every Thursday of the month Niarchos would fly from wherever he was, board his own *Creole,* and order the captain to go in tandem with the *Shemara.* Mrs. Ford was pleased to have Niarchos hanging about, and so was Mr. Basset. Stavros was gay and charming, and his special qualities shone over them all. A short while later, Charlotte discovered that she was pregnant.

Now, the first meeting between Henry Ford and Stavros Niarchos is lost to social history, but in the year before the *Shemara* and the *Creole* cruised the Mediterranean together, Ford and Niarchos had met and talked, and Niarchos had said that he was going to buy up a big block of Ford Motor Company stock. The hell you are, Ford had said, and Niarchos had said the hell he was not. Words flew, tempers did, too, and things were not convivial. Later, when Charlotte learned that she was pregnant, she called her father in Detroit, and he came to New York immediately. A father's anguish is a terrible thing, and Henry Ford did not like Stavros Niarchos, anyway. Ford spoke to his daughter and to his former wife, and at first the conferences were just among them, but then other McDonnells came along. What had happened was not unheard of, of course, not even in the nicest Irish Catholic families. Good girls got pregnant; it happened all the time, but this was bound to be so public, so painful and notorious. The years of priests, the days of instruction, the hours of prayer, the succeeding generations that had built up respectability, layer after layer, until sometimes it seemed that respectability had become the most important thing of all — now it was supposed to be left in tatters by a Greek. Furthermore, it was not even a nice Greek, a Greek they could trust, could recognize, or could coax into family ways. This was a Greek with four children by his third and present wife of eighteen years, a Greek thirty-two years older than Charlotte, and, unimaginably, eight years older than her father. In the way of big Irish families, everyone rallied round, offered suggestions, and did what they could. The problem was that they couldn't do anything.

Propriety had been the curse of the Irish ever since they had come to America. Once, the propriety had been reinforced by the faith, which made terrible the penalties for impropriety, but the old faith had been a comfort, offering answers to pain. When the old faith was weakened, worn away by legions of cloth-headed priests like Father Killeen and the conspiracy of time and wealth in America, the yearning for propriety had remained, at least among some of the Irish rich, and it had left in some of them a vacuity. In the year of Charlotte's anguish, a fund raiser for Georgetown University had approached one of her uncles, an alumnus, and asked him to give money.

"Absolutely not," Charlotte's uncle said. "Georgetown is

an overrated convent school, catering to Irish Catholic boys exclusively. Georgetown treats its young men like boys. My children will never go there." Charlotte's uncle was full of force and fury, retaliating for old wounds he probably didn't even know he had. "My money," he said, "will go to either Yale or Princeton because they provide the social training. Listen, I've been embarrassed when I've been asked what school I went to. Suppose there are two applications to the Links Club in New York, and one of the applicants is from Yale and the other from Georgetown. Now who do you think will get in?"

Charlotte's uncle was answering the question to his own satisfaction, and neatly managing to find all the wrong reasons for disliking the Jesuitical Georgetown. Snobbism without the old Irish guideposts to sustain it is only silly, and Charlotte and her family were coming into their anguish when all the old guideposts were being torn away. By 1965, America would not visit much opprobrium on a young unmarried woman who became pregnant, no matter how well known her name, and it would hardly be like the time Ingrid Bergman had found herself carrying a child by Roberto Rossellini and buffoons in Congress had stood up and denounced her as a threat to the public morality. Still, the family could not be quite sure of this, and Charlotte's mother, prompted by some odd impulse, even called Eugenia Niarchos. Mrs. Niarchos was not likely to be surprised by much after eighteen years of marriage to Stavros, but possibly this was beyond the bounds of anything that had ever happened before. Eugenia Niarchos, a genuinely nice lady, suffered it in silence. Mrs. Ford never talked about the call, either.

"The question," another of Charlotte's uncles said years later, "was who could we get to marry Charlotte?" There were lists of young men from good families, there were suggestions, there were moments of hope and days of darkness, and sometimes a curious exultation about the whole thing. This was natural; there is a residual joy among the Irish when they are going through their worst traumas, possibly because then they know they are up against something real. Charlotte's mother said that she would take her daughter to Switzerland, put her in one of those discreet places that always handled things so well, and let her have the baby there. Charlotte said no. No one in the family suggested an abortion. There were Catholic graces there still.

Curiously, there was another European coming into the family the same time as Niarchos. He was Giancarlo Uzielli, who was to marry Anne, Charlotte's modest and unassuming younger sister, and he had not been greeted by much enthusiasm, either. Uzielli, a stockbroker, had been married to a French actress. That marriage had ended in divorce, and Uzielli, who had been born a Jew but raised a Catholic, promised Anne that he would get a church annulment to go with the divorce. He could not get it in time for the marriage to Anne, however, and so he and Anne planned to be married by a judge on December 28, 1965. Anne asked for a priest to stand by them, and at least to give his blessing. In the family at the time, it had seemed like a critical problem.

The coming of Niarchos changed all that, bringing a tumult and crisis that could only be resolved one way: by marriage. Charlotte was adamant about it; her father was, too. Niarchos was given an ultimatum, and thinking that perhaps it was best this way after all, he capitulated. He divorced his wife and he met with Henry Ford in London, where, among other things, there were delicate financial matters to be worked out. Ford gave Charlotte a great deal of money, and Niarchos, in turn, put up a great deal of money that would go to his unborn child. Ford and Niarchos still did not like one another, but this, after all, was business. Subsequently, Niarchos gave Charlotte an engagement ring, which weighed forty carats, cost $600,000, and became known in the family as "the skating rink." Then he and Charlotte were married in Juarez, while Henry Ford, his daughter Anne said, "was about to have a heart attack." Nonetheless, they used Ford's plane to fly to Nassau, where Niarchos had a house, and then they chartered a Boeing 707 with 125 empty seats and flew to St. Moritz. They stayed there three months, and this, Charlotte said later, "was the only married life I ever had." Stavros, despite her pleadings, left her and went back to Eugenia. Charlotte was beaten, but not broken, and in time she recovered and married again. The family had rallied round her after the disaster with Stavros, and it had done it with its customary feelings of pride, anger, jealousy, defiance, and exhilaration. The family had always acted this way; it would do so again.

X

An Irish Requiem

IT WAS a great day for the Irish, or it was supposed to be, anyway, for the rich and historically minded among them were to be gathered together in the elegance of the Grand Ballroom of the Hotel Pierre in New York and given a chance to celebrate their heritage and put on the dog, too. The heritage had coursed down through the centuries, and the impulse to celebrate it was admirable. The idea of getting the rich, or at least the reasonably well off to do it, was implicit. The tickets to the dinner in the Grand Ballroom were $125 apiece, and Princess Grace of Monaco, who was once Grace Kelly of Philadelphia, was lending her patronage to the dinner to give it some tone. With tickets at $125, it was a little like the first Erina Ball in New York on St. Patrick's Day in 1831, when some of the Irish had restricted the guest list so that not all of the Irish could attend. The night of January 18, 1975, was not exactly like that, but the general idea was to summon up the socially prominent Irish and allow them to mingle with one another and with Princess Grace. That way they could confirm the contours of their own existence, and still applaud Ireland. This was a fine idea, and its execution told a good deal about the Irish and about what had happened to them in their years here. For one thing, it made it apparent that Irish Catholic society was dead, partly done in by its own success, and that you could hardly tell the Irish anymore from the

WASPs. By 1975, in the upper reaches of social prominence, they were virtually interchangeable.

The dinner at the Pierre was sponsored by the Irish American Cultural Institute, which had been founded in the unlikely place of St. Paul, Minnesota, in 1964 to promote the racial memories of the Irish. From the beginning, it had been largely a collaboration between two men, Dr. Eoin McKiernan, a scholar, and Patrick Butler, an amiable, unpretentious rich man, who had made a great deal of money in iron, gas, construction, and mining, and also married a Mott of the General Motors Motts, Mr. Butler's ancestors on both sides had come from County Wicklow in the Great Famine of '48 and settled first in Illinois and then in Minnesota, and possibly the best-known of all the Butlers after that was Pierce Butler, who was appointed to the Supreme Court of the United States in 1923. Patrick Butler, his relative from St. Paul, had gotten interested in Ireland because his people had come from there and because he had a love for fine horses. One of them, Untouchable, had won the Grand Prix at the Dublin Horse Show two years in a row. "Eoin McKiernan approached me with the idea of an Irish American Cultural Institute and I fell in with it right away," Mr. Butler says. "I have a friend from Ireland. He comes over here frequently, and he says he's convinced that 99 percent of the American Irish don't even know what counties their parents come from. They sing 'Mother Macree' and they get drunk on St. Patrick's Day. That's not really being Irish."

Mr. Butler was not necessarily talking about the rich and social Irish, although the thought is much the same. They are not much for singing "Mother Macree" and getting drunk on St. Patrick's Day, although some of them certainly do that, and their connection with Ireland has been of the most tangential kind. In 1966, before things began to change a little, this editorial appeared in the Irish *Times:*

The Irish in America for all their protestations of devotion to the "old sod," for all their St. Patrick's Day marching, for all their insistence on political intransigence on the home front in times of trouble — for all their love and loyalty, have done precious little in the matter of dollar subscription to activities in Ireland. We are often hearing of American bodies which are concerned with the restoration of Dublin's architecture. How much have they put down to rescue these properties? For years the Irish National Gallery lacked funds sufficient to enlarge the collection adequately. Who provided a capital sum? Not a sentimental Irish-American, but the mocking, ever critical George Bernard Shaw. When the Abbey Theatre was burnt down, what Irish-American offered to restore it? How many books and pictures from Irish writers and artists are bought in the United States? The Gaiety Theatre is likely to fall victim to the worship of the golden calf; what move has been made in America to help? We do not want this country to become an importunate poor relation; but the fact remains that almost nothing comes back to Ireland to give reality to the soft sayings of the Irish who have done well away; and if the benefactions of, say, the members of the Guinness family to Dublin are measured against the donations of millionaires who are far from the land, the ledger will have an almost virgin appearance on the American side.

The truth is that the rich American Irish have never identified much with Ireland. For one thing, Ireland was the place their grandparents had fled, fleeing not by choice, but because the land was barren. No one wanted to look back at it. For another thing, there has been something incongruous in America in being rich and Irish. There has always been that hint of scorn, that touch of derision, that suggestion of laughter directed at the Irish rich. If one is rich in America, it is usually better to forget about being Irish, too. In the 1970s, consequently, the rich American Irish were not identifying much with Ireland, but more importantly they were not even identifying with one another. It was really extraordinary. The golden boys and girls of yesterday had clung together not so much because they were enchanted by one .another, but because they had been raised that way. Their mothers and fathers and uncles and aunts had clung together, too, protecting the faith, keeping things in the family, and seldom straying far from other Irish Catholics. Perhaps they preferred it this way; perhaps they were afraid to have it any other way. Whatever the reasons, they had set up a separate society, rejecting the WASPs before the WASPs could reject them, and simultaneously doing all the things in their society that the WASPs were doing in theirs. The separate society had worked, and the Irish Catholic families that swam to its top kept on going, never looked back, and soon became just like WASPs. Besides, by the 1970s the children of the rich Irish Catholics had made too many marriages outside the fold; too many things had happened to them, and the church, the glue that had always held Irish Catholic society together, was in a hell of a shape. The church had new voices and visions, and in place of a nicely ordered, neatly determined world, the Irish Catholics now had a multiplicity of choices offered them. The tight little islands on which the rich Irish Catholics had stranded themselves, or been stranded by others, were disappearing. The old morality was still around; so were the old ways of doing things, but the rich Irish Catholics who did them were not the ones who got into the gossip columns. The ones who got into the gossip columns had turned into something else. You couldn't recognize them as Irish Catholics.

Moreover, what was left of the Irish connection, when there was anything left at all, was usually ersatz. A few years ago, Mr. and Mrs. Daniel Moran gave a St. Patrick's Day party in Palm Beach. Mrs. Moran was a former New York showgirl, who had married and then been widowed by Horace Dodge, and then had married Danny Moran, a New York cop. The tabloids were full of it. Mrs. Moran is a generous woman, and when she set out to give the St. Patrick's Day party she invited 500 guests, set up striped tents outside her house on the ocean, and decorated everything inside the tents green. Each guest had a place card with his name written on it in green ink, and each place card was stuck into a potato that had been hollowed out and filled with shamrocks. Mrs. Moran even wore a new green dress. Everyone who was anyone in Palm Beach was there, and Mrs. Moran saved the decorations because the next night she was going to give a party for her son, who had just been baptized a Catholic by Monsignor O'Mahaney of St. Edward's Church.

St. Edward's is the most Irish Catholic of places. It was built by, and named after, Colonel Edward Riley Bradley, that nearly legendary Palm Beach gambler and philanthropist, and in the beginning it had been run by the Jesuits. There was a time when all the rich Irish Catholics went to Palm Beach, staying at the Breakers Hotel and going to Mass at St. Edward's, and so the church had become a very profitable operation. Consequently, the local diocese had waged a fierce, internecine war with the Jesuits and taken it over. Until his retirement, Monsignor O'Mahaney was its pastor, and for years in Palm Beach he was something like the chairman of the board for the rich Irish Catholics who took their ease there. He was, and is, full of "faith and bygorys," and not long ago a visitor, who assumed the answer would be County Wicklow, say, or County Cork, asked Monsignor O'Mahaney where he had been born. "Me bye," Monsignor O'Mahaney said, "I was born in this great country — in Lawrence, Massachusetts." Still, even with so much that was apparently Irish hovering about, there was nothing that was truly Irish at Mrs. Moran's St. Patrick's Day party. The green decorations, the green ink, the potatoes filled with shamrocks were caricatures, harmless ones, but, as Mr. Butler said, "That's not really being Irish."

The Irish American Cultural Institute wanted none of this; it wanted the authentic and not the ersatz at the Pierre, and in a way it got it because it did things in an authentic Irish American way. Some of the invitations to the dinner were sent out with a small picture of Princess Grace accompanying them. She looked regal in the picture, the way she always does, wearing a tiara, a sash, and a couple of decorations from the principality of Monaco, but it was not classy to hawk her picture about this way, no matter how much you wanted people to know she would be the guest of honor. Worse, on the back of the picture, just above where it said, "Her Serene Highness," it said, "Souvenir."

If the pictures had been just a little larger, with perhaps a black border around them, they would have looked exactly like what inspired them in the first place — Mass cards. It was an authentic Irish Catholic touch, but not one that would delight the nominally Irish, nominally Catholic, ladies on the Upper East Side of New York or in the more expensive suburbs. They had put things like that behind them long ago, and the invitations did not get even as far as the silver or Lowestoft bowls where the ladies piled up their invitations. The invitations were ignored, and indeed one notable thing about the dinner at the Pierre was not who was there, but who was not. There were no Murrays or McDonnells, and no descendants of Thomas Fortune Ryan, or of John and James Cavanagh of Boston, or of many of the other old Irish Catholic grandees. There was only one Grace, and he was from California, not from among the Graces who lived in and around New York. The Irish who had made it big in a social way did not show up to mix in with the Irish who had not, and looking around the Pierre at dinner that night an Irishman who wanted to be elsewhere said, "The real action tonight is at

Marian Javits'. She's giving a party for George Weidenfeld."

Now Mrs. Javits is the wife of the Senator, and Sir George Weidenfeld is the British publisher, and they are both Jewish. Old Thomas E. Murray would have been uncomfortable at Mrs. Javits', but his descendants were not, and at least one of them passed up the Pierre to be there that night. Moreover, Governor Hugh Carey was an honorary chairman of the dinner at the Pierre, but he didn't come, and neither did Senator Edward Kennedy, who was supposed to, and neither did any member of the Kennedy family. It had also been announced that some celebrities of greater or lesser talent would be at the dinner, but they didn't show up, either. The most surprising thing, however, was that Terence Cardinal Cooke didn't make it. Cardinal Spellman would have been there if he had been alive, and if things had been the way they were, say, thirty years before, Cardinal Spellman would have taken the dinner and made it his own. Instead, the Irish American Cultural Institute got a couple of bishops, one of whom said grace and the other of whom pronounced the benediction.

Furthermore, the last Hearst newspaper had disappeared from New York years before, and so the press didn't say much about the dinner, even though squads of paparazzi showed up for Princess Grace. On the afternoon of the dinner she visited Waterloo Village, New Jersey, a Colonial restoration, to dedicate a plaque in the memory of 1100 Irish who built a canal there in 1825. The Irish American Cultural Institute had announced the visit with a flurry of press releases and phone calls, and said that Princess Grace would be at Waterloo Village under its auspices. A society columnist in the New York *Daily News* wrote something about this in her column, mentioning a good deal about Waterloo Village and Princess Grace and hardly anything about the Irish part of it. The chairman of the arrangements for the Irish American Cultural Institute, a businessman from Short Hills, New Jersey, was infuriated by this, and said that the society columnist had missed the point. In fact, it was the businessman who had missed the point. Society columnists in the 1970s weren't interested in how the Irish celebrated themselves, or where they had come from. The press will pay a great deal of attention to Governor Carey's Irish background, just as it did to President Kennedy's, and Governor Carey will be a willing accomplice, frequently mentioning the Irish connection himself. Kennedy frequently did, too. This is because being Irish suits a politician; it explains things about him, crediting him with more of a sense of humor than he probably has, and lending him a certain flair. (Senator James Buckley of New York is an exception. None of the Buckleys ever mentions Ireland at all.) To be identifiably Irish, however, and to be allowed to be socially prominent, out of the top drawer, as they say, is something else again.

Princess Grace, the daughter of an energetic and imaginative father who had once been a bricklayer, then an Olympic rowing champion, and finally a very rich man, is Irish, but in the eyes of columnists and other arbiters she has somehow passed beyond it. Her father's grandfather emigrated to Vermont, becoming the only Democrat in the town where he settled, and the story is that he was arrested for stuffing the ballot box one election day because when the ballot box was opened there were two Democratic votes in it. Princess Grace is the true-born queen of the Irish Catholics (Rose Kennedy is the dowager empress), even though she is hardly ever thought of as being Irish. Probably she never thinks of herself as being Irish, either, and her appearance at the dinner of the Irish American Cultural Institute may have been inspired as much by the apparent desire of her brother, John, to enter politics as it was by any rediscovery of ethnicity. Indeed, Princess Grace seldom visits Ireland, and while this is hardly a true test of whether you are Irish or not, it is something of an indication of how close your ties are to the place.

Mrs. Kennedy has not spent much time in Ireland, either.

She was there with her father in 1908, and thirty years later, after her husband was appointed Ambassador to the Court of St. James's, the ship carrying her to England stopped first at the Port of Cóbh. If Mrs. Kennedy has been back there since it has not been reported. Nonetheless, Mrs. Kennedy has never forgotten who she is, nor, for that matter, could she. She is an Irish Catholic lady, one of the last great ones, and like her old friend Anna McDonnell she endures, trusting in her faith, Cardinal Newman's "Meditations," and the Stations of the Cross, and carrying them before her like a torch. In 1952, Pope Pius XII made her a Papal Countess, the only time he conferred that honor on anyone during his long reign, and on the scroll that Cardinal Spellman presented to Mrs. Kennedy announcing the title it said that she was being hailed for her "exemplary life . . . and many charities." Mrs. Kennedy has indeed led an exemplary life, and her husband gave many millions to Catholic charities, and among all the words that have been written about the Kennedys and what made them not enough have mentioned her. Irish Catholic society is matriarchal, and it is the mother who passes on the values, as well as the fears, guilts, and strivings from one generation to the next. It was not Joe Kennedy who held the family together; it was always Rose, and the impulses that turned other Irish Catholics into WASPs turned her into a monument to Irish Catholic motherhood. Her autobiography is an exercise in dignity, very nearly Victorian, and orchestrated to the rhythm of propriety and success. Somewhere in it she cautions her grandchildren to remember that they are descended from poor immigrants, and this is gracious because it is something that most rich American Irish forget. Nonetheless, at a dinner party in Palm Beach a few years ago, Mrs. Kennedy remarked that her family, the Fitzgeralds, was also descended from kings of old Ireland. It is possible that the Fitzgeralds were, but the fact that she should even mention it tells something about Mrs. Kennedy.

Rose Kennedy was well into her adult years before she met many Protestants. As a young woman, she lived in a society so segregated that, when the Boston newspapers reported social activities, they carefully put the stories about Protestants in one part of the paper and stories about Catholics in another. Young Catholic women in Boston had their Cecilian Club; young Protestant women had the Junior League. When Protestant met Catholic it was by chance, and when Mrs. Kennedy once engaged a Protestant pediatrician it was a small scandal. For years, Rose Kennedy never complained out loud about this, and she talked about the separation of Protestant and Catholic as if it had been nothing more than a social convention, silly and arbitrary perhaps, but certainly nothing to be resented. And yet . . . and yet. A Murray talked to her about it once, and Mrs. Kennedy dismissed it, saying that as a young woman she had paid no attention to the separate societies. Her life, she said, had been full of compensation and pleasure, and she had had no resentment about ever being excluded from anything. And yet . . . The striking thing about Rose Kennedy is her propriety; it is almost as legendary as her faith, and for years it has been her weapon against the Boston society that excluded her. Once, it was a commonplace for biographers and feature writers to talk about the Kennedys' drive for excellence, their competitive spirit and their quest for success, and to say that it was a consequence of Joe Kennedy's fierce ambitions. Joe Kennedy was fiercely ambitious, all right, but he was just never at home much of the time. Rose was; she was at home all the time, and she suffered all the little social outrages. She has never forgotten any of them.

There was no way to conquer Protestant Beacon Hill (or Protestant Bronxville, where the Kennedys also lived) except to be better than the people who lived there. Rose Kennedy insisted on being better; she insisted that her children be better. It was her revenge. She also insisted on the Catholic pieties far more than her husband ever did. When her daughter Kathleen, "Kick," married the Protestant Marquess of Hartington, Rose Kennedy declined to attend the ceremony. Joe Kennedy wanted to go, to give the couple a kind of fatherly blessing, but Rose Kennedy said no. She could not do otherwise. Joe Kennedy wanted the children, especially the boys, to have secular educations. His wife insisted on Catholic educations, and this, she says, was one of the few arguments they ever had. (There were others, of course, Kathleen's marriage being only one.) Subsequently, Joe Jr., the oldest son, escaped Catholic schools entirely. Jack had part of a year at Canterbury, Bobby a year at Portsmouth Priory, and Teddy a term at Portsmouth Priory and then a term at Cranwell, a Jesuit school in Lenox, Massachusetts. None of the boys was particularly happy at Catholic schools. Bobby came closest, but the year at Portsmouth Priory was all that even he could handle. The Kennedy girls went entirely to Catholic schools, beginning, naturally, at Sacred Heart convents. This suited Joe Kennedy fine. It is doubtful that he cared much where the girls were educated, or even that they were educated at all. This was part of the Irish Catholic tradition, too. The country is full of women from prominent Irish Catholic families who have never seen the inside of a college or university, and whose daughters are beginning to taste academe only now. None of old Thomas E. Murray's daughters ever went to college; few of his many granddaughters did, even fleetingly, and it is only now that some, though hardly all, of his great-granddaughters are attending. For years, the threnody among Catholic intellectuals was about the absence of Catholic writers, scientists, and artists. It might just as well have been about the absence of educated Irish Catholic women. There has always been this curious trait about the Irish Catholic culture: the women have been the custodians of its values, but there has been a holy horror among them about appearing brighter than the men. Perhaps it is because the men couldn't stand it. Perhaps it is because there is a tacit recognition among them that, while the women would run things, the men would appear to be in charge. When Thomas E. Murray died in 1929, the letter writer to the *Times* had said that a flag flying at half-staff was really "a banner proclaiming the love of a boy for his mother." The letter writer was correct, more so than he thought, and mingled with the love of Irish boys for their mothers has always been a great deal of fear.

"The primary agent of . . . seduction by responsibility is the Irish mother," Father Andrew M. Greeley, the Irish American sociologist, writes. "The Jewish mother may kill her children with kindness . . . The Irish mother manipulates her children by starving them for affection. The Jewish mother may, according to her sons who write about her, say, 'Eat your chicken soup, it's good for you.' But the Irish mother announces, 'There is not enough chicken soup to go around; and if you don't love mother enough you'll go to bed hungry.'" Therefore, there is a compulsion on Irish boys to please their mothers; they have to. There is a compulsion to be so eminently respectable that all of mother's hopes and dreams will be realized. The mechanism for this is the same among the families of subway motormen from the Bronx as it is among the families of great financiers from Boston. Joe Kennedy may have been mean and tough; he may have pushed and prodded his sons. And yet . . . there was Rose. The successful Boston Irish considered themselves successful only by the standards that the Protestants set for them. In fact, these Protestant Brahmins were not much more than the fag ends of the once vibrant Puritan tradition, and they were debilitated by years of clipping coupons and maintaining their own respectability. They were not much to emulate, but the Boston Irish emulated them anyway, fearful that if they did not they would have no identity of their own. They would waste away, dry up, and be swept out on the Charles. Beacon Hill never did accept the Irish, although it tolerated men like William Cardinal O'Connell, who walked so easily among the bankers and merchants and made their ways his ways, but O'Connell, after all, had a red hat. Rose Kennedy had no red hat, but she had respectability and she had all those children. The sons among them would prosper and be famous. They would have to; they would be Rose Kennedy's revenge.

"Some see the tragedy of the Kennedy family as hideous coincidence," Father Greeley writes. "Others see it as an ugly fate; but one who knows the Irish is inclined to suspect that the clan Kennedy, like so many other Irish clans, is damned by its own self-destructive instincts." The self-destructive urge, he says, comes from the Irish habit of sublimating their own best instincts, and of fighting so hard to be accepted that they never become themselves. Father Greeley says that the Irish Catholic mother is the agent for all this, although when he talks of the Kennedys' self-destructive quality he is disinclined to mention Mrs. Kennedy. It would be to say the unsayable if he did. But Rose Kennedy was heir to, and perpetuator of, a tradition, and she could not have been anything else.

James T. Farrell knew all about Irish self-destruction when he wrote the Studs Lonigan books. Eugene O'Neill understood it when he wrote *Long Day's Journey into Night*. John O'Hara always understood it, although he never truly explored it. Joseph P. Kennedy, Jr., a bomber pilot during World War II, twice refused to be sent home although he had the required hours of flying time, and he died when his Liberator bomber, laden with explosives, blew up over the English Channel. Jack Kennedy suffered a variety of illnesses as a child, some of them apparently psychosomatic, and after his PT boat had been cut in half by a Japanese destroyer, he decided, bad back and all, to swim miles through dangerous waters for help. Later, against the advice of the Secret Service, he rode through the streets of Dallas without the bubbletop protection on his car. Ted Kennedy's life has been a series of smaller and larger tragedies, and he seems to suffer, like so many Irish, from paroxysms of bravado. During his brother's presidential campaign in 1960, Ted Kennedy, speaking in Wisconsin, found himself at a ski-jumping meet near Madison. He had never jumped before, but somehow he found himself going down the Olympic-size runway. Somehow he landed upright without breaking his neck. A few months later, at a rodeo in Miles City, Montana, he rode a bucking bronco out of a chute. He had never done that before, either, and his family all seemed to regard it with some pride. The question is, why did the Kennedys have to try so hard? What is it they were always trying to prove?

For one thing, they were always trying to prove that they were as good as Beacon Hill, and whether they knew it or not it left them with a feeling of anger. In an odd way, it left them with a feeling of guilt, too. The Irish mother has always tried to keep her sons close to her, and she wants them to be respectable. In the Kennedys' case this meant that they should run for high office. There is nothing more respectable or praiseworthy than that (or a better way of getting back at Beacon Hill), although high office can separate a son from his mother and make him feel guilty about it. Worse, in her untiring search for respectability, Rose Kennedy has always seemed inclined to the belief that a Kennedy's personal behavior, any Kennedy's personal behavior, has somehow been beyond reproach. Years ago, for example, a Murray girl had a husband who was never particularly faithful to his marriage vows, and once or twice he slipped off for a rendezvous with one of Mrs. Kennedy's then unmarried daughters. Mrs. Kennedy heard of it, and full of wrath approached the Murray girl and demanded to know why she had allowed such a thing to happen. Possibly she should have asked her daughter instead.

More recently, there was Chappaquiddick. Whatever the sequence of events that night, it was tacky before it was tragic, and it is not edifying to think of a bunch of middle-aged, married men (Ted Kennedy was the youngest) partying in the sand dunes with an equal number of unmarried, much younger women. It had all the elegance of a beer bust given by fraternity boys, but in her autobiography Mrs. Kennedy says it was a "cookout," held only to pay off some political obligations that Teddy had incurred in his last campaign. Whatever it was, it was hardly that, but Rose Kennedy will preserve the appearance of respectability no matter what. The problem is that this can be hell on a son or daughter, particularly a son, because then he feels bad about betraying Mother's trust. Irish Catholic mothers seldom blame their sons for indiscretions, preferring to blame their wives, instead, and when Mrs. Kennedy speaks of some of Ted Kennedy's misfortunes she sometimes forgets to mention that his wife, Joan, has suffered some, too. Indeed, Joan Kennedy's personal problems must be a particularly hard cross for Rose Kennedy to bear because the problems have been announced so publicly. Beacon Hill would never have done that; it would have been against the rules. Rose Kennedy does not like it. (When Teddy announced to his mother that he wanted to marry Joan, Mrs. Kennedy immediately called her friend Mother O'Byrne of Manhattanville College, where Joan was a student. She wanted to know about her grades and "behavior.") Having betrayed Mother's trust so often, and worse, not having Mother blame him for it, Ted Kennedy is a very guilty man. His guilt breeds anger, and the anger turns into self-hatred. It is a curse of the Irish. Ted Kennedy raises hell with himself, putting either his career or physical well-being in jeopardy, and when he has punished himself sufficiently, or made a fool of himself sufficiently, then he returns to home, hearth, and, symbolically, to Mother. He is a true-born son of the Irish.

There were true-born children of the Irish at the dinner of the Irish American Cultural Institute, too, and for the most part they were pleasant people, all eager to have a good time. When Princess Grace appeared she was mobbed, and second- and third-generation Irish American businessmen and their wives pressed in all about her, hoping to turn up in one of the pictures that undoubtedly would appear the next day in *Women's Wear Daily* or the *Daily News*. There was noise, there was laughter, there was confusion, but somehow there was no fizz to the champagne; it was flat. A pipe band marched into the Grand Ballroom, and although the pipers wore MacKenzie tartans, which were Scottish and not Irish, no one seemed to mind, or for that matter even to notice. Soon the master of ceremonies stood up and asked if someone had lost a $5000 bill. He said that anyone who knew the serial number could reclaim it. No one laughed much, but the master of ceremonies pressed on and introduced a bishop, who prayed for "the little green isle of saints and scholars." An Irishman from Dublin, who just happened to be in New York that night, looked around him and said not unkindly, but really too loudly, "They've all become the thing they hate the most — respectable." A few people glared at him.

Later, the master of ceremonies introduced the Bunratty Singers. They were attractive young women who sing for the tourists at Bunratty Castle near Shannon Airport, and they had been flown to New York by the Irish Tourist Board. The master of ceremonies introduced them as solemnly as if he were introducing the Pope. For no particular reason then, the man from Dublin looked up, and again not unkindly, but still too loudly, said, "Where are all the Irish pagans? My God, the place is festooned with priests." Soon the master of ceremonies told all the women in the Grand Ballroom to turn to another woman and tell her the date of her birthday. He said that the woman with the birthday closest to that of Princess Grace would win a prize. He waited for the women to tell one another, and then, beaming, he said that Princess Grace's birthday was November 12. "Bricklayers' Day," the man from Dublin shouted, and then he had a thought. "Do you know," he said, "that I've never laid a brick in me life?" The American Irish sitting near him did not think this was very funny, although a few other people did, and soon a young man from Boston, fairly trembling with rage, walked over to the man from Dublin. "Slob," he said, "if you slobs didn't want to come here, why did you come?" Then the young man from Boston sat down.

Slowly, with a feeling of pain, the evening began to come to an end. There were speeches, and everyone at the head table was introduced. There was a raffle, and someone won a trip to Ireland. Princess Grace said it had been "an auspicious evening," and a bishop said they had all "served a noble cause." Everyone's speeches seemed longer than they probably were, and ennui was everywhere. Respectability was everywhere, too, and the guests did not seem to be having a particularly good time. Possibly they wondered why they were there, or whether, because they were Irish, they were supposed to behave some other way than they did. When it was finally over, the master of ceremonies said, "Thank you one and all, and good night," and as everyone filed out of the Grand Ballroom the band played "Hello, Dolly." A vocalist sang the lyrics then — in French.

XI

Profit and Loss

PETER MCDONNELL, Anna McDonnell's father-in-law, had come to this country from County Longford during the Great Famine and become what was called a bondsman. The McDonnells, when they recall him now, say he was a travel agent, and in a way he was because he was responsible for transporting an uncounted number of other Irishmen to America and seeing that they stayed there. New York law said that the immigrants could not become public charges, and so the bondsman would sell the immigrants bonds, frequently when they stepped off the gangplank. The bonds guaranteed that the bondsman would care for the immigrants when they fell on hard times, although the bondsman hardly ever did this, and bonding was as corrupt and shady a business as went on in New York. The other thing the bondsman did was to recruit men in Ireland for labor gangs in America. Bonding was never a nice business, but it was usually a profitable one, and Peter McDonnell did nicely in it. It was his son James who married Anna Murray and founded McDonnell & Company.

McDonnell & Company was a brokerage house, and the supposition about brokerage houses is that a man must be intelligent to get ahead in one. There are intelligent men on Wall Street, but intelligence has never been a prerequisite in the merchandising of securities, and sometimes it can be a hindrance, causing a man to wonder what got him into such a profession in the first place. If he is candid, he will admit he did it only to make money and that this is perhaps enough for him. James McDonnell went into the brokerage business simply for that reason, and he said that he wanted to make a million dollars by the time he was married, and then another millions dollars for each of his children. He did this easily, and when he died in 1958 at the age of seventy-eight, McDonnell & Company was flourishing. It was not the biggest brokerage house, but it seemed to be one of the most stable, and from the beginning it had prospered because Mr. McDonnell understood about rights. There were always brokerage houses that specialized in particular stocks, but not that many that specialized in rights, and James McDonnell, realizing that he was into something good, went in for them.

A right is a document that allows a shareholder to buy additional shares of stock in a company within a specified time at a specified price. Suppose, for instance, that a right allows a shareholder to buy a share of stock for $10 at any time in the next six months. Suppose that the stock doubles in price to $20. If the shareholder buys 1000 shares at $10 apiece, spending $10,000, his stock will be worth $20,000, and he will have made a $10,000 profit. Suppose, however, that someone had speculated in the rights themselves, buying each one for $1. For $1000, he would still have the privilege of buying the 1000 shares at $10 apiece. Therefore, if the stocks went to $20 he could buy them for $10,000, add the $1000 that the rights cost, and make a profit of $9000 on the original investment. Of course, if the stocks depreciated in value so that they were worth less than $10, the rights would be worthless. Still, in that case the investor would have lost only the $1000 that the rights cost. Obviously, there was enormous money to be made in rights. They were all so simple, and a quick-witted broker who dealt in them could make a maxi-

mum profit with only a minimum effort. James McDonnell
was sure of it.

Consequently, McDonnell made money, and for years
money ran through the family as a leitmotif. The McDonnells
did not really sow, but they did reap, and in that big tribe of
Irish Catholics to which they belonged they were easily the
richest. When James McDonnell died, the company was almost the family's private treasury. Three McDonnell sons
were connected with it, and on the death of the father, one of
the sons, T. Murray McDonnell, became the head of McDonnell & Company. He was thirty-seven years old.

Precisely what drove Murray nobody knew, although he
had married the daughter of Horace Flanigan, the chairman
of Manufacturers Hanover Trust, and he seemed to have a
great fondness for the lush life. Possibly, too, he wanted glory.
He rode to hounds from his house in Peapack, New Jersey,
owned and bred thoroughbred horses, and in time became
major-domo to Mrs. Jacqueline Kennedy Onassis. Murray
and his wife frequently entertained Mrs. Onassis and her children at their home in Peapack, and sometimes without meaning to they entertained the neighbors, too. "Murray would
invite you for dinner," one of them said, "and tell you that
Jackie was going to arrive at eight, and so we should all arrive
fifteen minutes before that. Jesus, you would have thought it
was the Queen of England." In his way, Murray became very
grand, and on taking over McDonnell & Company he began to
make that very grand, too. When James McDonnell died, the
brokerage house had its main office at 254 Park Avenue, with
branch offices in Chicago, Detroit, and Asbury Park, New
Jersey. Murray, however, chose to expand, and he opened
office after office until there were twenty-six of them, including one in Paris. One brother, Charles, or "Bishie," as he was
known in the family, disagreed with the way Murray was running things and decided to resign from McDonnell & Com-

pany. No matter, Murray pressed on. Besides having the blessing of Mrs. Onassis, he had the blessing of the church, and he was a financial adviser to the Archdiocese of New York. His life was going well, and it was not apparent that Murray was simply not much of a businessman, or at least that he was a better salesman than manager, and far better equipped at making money than in knowing what to do with it. This, incidentally, is an old failing of the Irish.

Nobody knows exactly when the trouble started at McDonnell & Company, but in retrospect it seems to have begun in the early 1960s, when the big boom was under way on Wall Street and the brokerage houses were doing more business than they could really handle. They began to have what the financial press called back-office problems, which meant that the clerks and bookkeepers in the brokerage houses got so inundated with pieces of paper that they could no longer keep up. Wall Street was still run like something out of Dickens, and people hunched over desks, wrote out orders and confirmations, and in general behaved as if electronics and automation were as remote as the possibility of landing a man on the moon. Before the war, a million shares might be traded on a big day on the New York Stock Exchange. By the early 1960s, there were days when 10 million shares were traded, and soon there would be 15- and even 20-million share days. The back offices had to be automated; they were losing control.

In 1962, McDonnell & Company began to put computers in its back office. The computers, however, weren't up to the job, and the back office still fell behind. Year by year, although no one seemed to know it, McDonnell & Company sank into chaos, slowly at first, and then with increasing speed. Stocks were bought, and then never delivered. Dividends weren't paid. Pieces of paper got lost. In 1968, McDonnell & Company later admitted, it overestimated by $91.8 million the amount of securities that its customers had on deposit. It also had some $9 million worth of securities that didn't seem to belong to anyone, or at least no one whom McDonnell & Company could identify. The place was in a sorry mess, and the wonder is that the Stock Exchange didn't step in and suspend McDonnell & Company from trading before it did. But Wall Street has always been run like a locker room, and stockbrokers who keep seeing one another in places like Southampton take pains not to cause one another embarrassment. McDonnell & Company stayed in business. In 1968, the *Wall Street Journal* reported that McDonnell & Company's revenue reached $33 million, although its profit was only $440,000. Even the $440,000 figure was suspect, however, because by 1968 no one seemed to have any true idea of what was going on. The operation was coming apart, and then there was something even worse. Sean McDonnell, the youngest son of Anna McDonnell, died.

By general agreement, Sean was his mother's favorite. According to family legend, he was also the most competent of the McDonnells, and the man who one day would be best suited to run McDonnell & Company. He had gone to Fordham rather than Georgetown because he had preferred living at home, and then he had gone to Harvard Business School, married a girl who was both suitable and pretty, and entered McDonnell & Company as a senior vice president. Then, on a June day, while he was jogging near his home in Greenwich, Connecticut, he had a heart attack and died. He was thirty-three years old. It is possible that Sean was never as capable at business as his family thought he was, and when he died he was in charge of the daily operations of McDonnell & Company, which meant that he had made as many bad decisions there as anyone. Still, there was something else about Sean, and it was the quality that truly did make his mother cherish him most of all. In a letter to his wife, he once wrote this:

You shouldn't worry; just put me in the hands of the Lord and say: "Thy will be done." The good Lord has smiled on us so often — so trust Him. We are all in His hands. The most difficult thing in the world, sometimes, is to believe that what He does, or lets happen, is for the best, but it is. Pray often; put yourself in the presence of God; say "hi" often.

Even if Sean had lived there is no reason to think that things would have been different at McDonnell & Company, but his death contributed to the final unhinging. In January of 1969, Lawrence O'Brien, who was then the chairman of the Democratic National Committee, was brought in as chairman of the company. Whatever his other virtues, O'Brien was a man with absolutely no experience on Wall Street, and it was hard to see what he would lend McDonnell & Company other than his name, or perhaps the appearance of power and political influence. The appearance of power has always counted for something on Wall Street, and for years one of the great assets of McDonnell & Company was Henry Ford, Murray McDonnell's brother-in-law. The assumption was that the fortunes of McDonnell & Company were somehow bound in with the fortunes of the Ford Motor Company, and that the integrity of the one had something to do with that of the other. In a way this was true, and among the McDonnells it was known that Murray had borrowed $1 million from Henry when things had begun to go sour. Then Ford's marriage had begun to go sour, too, and he had declined to lend more. With Ford out, Larry O'Brien was in, and his appointment was loudly announced, although his departure seven months later was a good deal quieter. Murray may only have been trying to broaden his political spectrum when he hired the Democratic O'Brien because in Nixon's Republican White House he had a friend, too. This was his brother-in-law Peter Flanigan, who assisted Mr. Nixon in a variety of ways, some of which the

Democrats found questionable. Once, on the floor of the Senate, Thomas Eagleton of Missouri worked himself into a state and said that "Peter Flanigan is no mere patcher of plaster, no apprentice applier of Band-Aids. Rather, there is evidence to believe that he is the mastermind, the possessor of the scuttling feet that are heard, faintly, retreating into the distance in the wake of a White House ordered cave-in to some giant corporation." Press Secretary Ron Ziegler said it wasn't so, and anyway it didn't matter to McDonnell & Company because not even the faintest of scuttlers could have saved it. Murray McDonnell's dreams of glory were fading, and at about the same time that Larry O'Brien was entering and leaving the business, McDonnell & Company was shutting down twenty-three of its twenty-six offices, dismissing 1200 of its 1500 employees, reducing the salaries of the ones who were left, and even closing the executive dining room. Nothing helped, even though Murray, who still kept his limousine, was professing to believe that he could get out of all his difficulties. A new man came in to run the daily operations, and he was a chip off the old block, too. He had been an executive of the old Irish Catholic Grace & Company, and he had also managed money for the church. He didn't help, either; nor, for that matter, could he. In 1969, McDonnell & Company had a ten-month operating loss of $6.5 million.

Much of the family's money was being drained away, particularly that of Anna McDonnell and her daughter Anne, who was now married to Dean Johnson, a California lawyer. Moreover, a good deal of money that belonged to Murray's wife was also invested in McDonnell & Company. Murray announced that he was going to negotiate a loan for his failing company, and that the loan would come from a group headed by Dan Lufkin of Donaldson, Lufkin & Jenrette. Lufkin was a friend (later he and Murray would renovate a fine old Georgian house in Ireland together) and he was a relative as well. His Aunt Marie, Mrs. Elgood Lufkin, was a daughter of old Thomas E. Murray. Actually, Murray McDonnell was staying with his roots, moving in a small circle of Irish Catholics the way his grandfather, father, and uncles always had, only this time it was all going wrong, terribly wrong, and the circle was falling apart. Even the loan from Dan Lufkin never materialized, and on March 12, 1970, Murray McDonnell announced that McDonnell & Company was closing down. It even owed its customers money, although the books were in such bad shape that nobody knew how much. A month later, the Securities and Exchange Commission filed a suit charging that Murray, in trying to raise money to save things, had made "untrue statements of material facts" when he had tried to sell stock in McDonnell & Company to his own employees. It was a charge Murray chose not to contest.

The collapse of McDonnell & Company did not end things for the McDonnells. After all, families do not simply collapse, although they do change their characters, and certainly they change their preoccupations. Some of the McDonnells had married well. Some of them still had their old connections. Some of them even had a trace of old Thomas E. Murray's energy, but for a generation of them now the mood was sour. Money had always been important to the Irish who had had it, for with money there was security and status, and the Irish needed these desperately. Thomas E. Murray, being of a different sensibility than some of his heirs, had found his security and status in work and the church. His children and grandchildren had the church, but their work was not so productive as his, and so they had begun to measure themselves by their houses and bank accounts. Once, an engineering colleague of Thomas E. Murray's had set out to write that great man's biography, and in it he had decided to say something about his money. "Above all he was not preoccupied in build-

ing up a corruption fund for his descendants," the engineer
wrote quaintly. "He feared lest that would take away from
them the best incentives to make something really worthwhile
of their lives."

Murray, of course, was an old-fashioned man, steeped in
the verities that had held so many of the Irish together while
they scrambled up from poverty and into comfort and riches.
His daughter Anna believed in the old verities, too, and if she
was grieved by the loss of McDonnell & Company she hardly
showed it. It was an annoyance certainly, but hardly a catas-
trophe, and Anna went on the way she always had — firmly,
resolutely, and with her mind fixed on God's mysteries. "I
never doubted my faith, never," she said not long before she
died. She was in her apartment on Fifth Avenue, and the
apartment, done years before by McMillen, suited her. Long
after you left it you remembered highly polished surfaces and
the oil painting of a pope that hung on a wall. "My brothers
and sisters went to Mass and holy communion every day,"
Mrs. McDonnell said. "My father set an example for us. We
were raised in the faith, a living faith. Nothing has ever hin-
dered that in me for one instant." Then, musing aloud really,
she said that many things had changed in her lifetime, that
families didn't stay together the way they once did, that parents didn't pass on a system of values the way they once had,
and that when children went out into the world now they
weren't as well equipped for it as once they had been. While
she spoke she looked at a picture of her granddaughters Charlotte and Anne. She didn't talk about them, but they must
have been on her mind, and it was as if she had passed judg-
ment on her own children and then her children's children.
She had not necessarily found them wanting, but she knew
they were not like she was, and the truth was that it didn't
seem to matter to her much. Anna McDonnell was a survivor,
not likely to mourn what could not be helped, and she had

transcended her past simply by being faithful to it. She had never looked back, never grieved outwardly, and when her son Murray fell from grace after McDonnell & Company collapsed and his brothers and sisters scorned him, she would have none of it. She stayed close to Murray, and chided her other children for not taking his side.

True, the loss of the money meant that she had to curtail her style of living, but with the help of her daughter Anne and her granddaughter Charlotte she never really dismantled it, and she fretted only because she could no longer give the sums to the church that she once had. Her father would have understood that perfectly. The church had held together generations of the Irish, and no other immigrant group ever had its behavior so perfectly complemented by its religion. Thomas E. Murray made the Stations of the Cross every morning with perfect discipline, and if he felt uncertainties about anything it never showed. Anna was the same way; many of her contemporaries were, too, and by persistence and discipline they lifted the Irish out of the immigrant class and made them acceptable to the other Americans.

The Irish had dug ditches at first. Then some of them had discovered gold and silver, built San Francisco, become a part of the Gilded Age, run up fortunes on Wall Street, and operated political machines. But they had never been accepted the way the rich Protestants were, and so they had gone it alone. Perhaps the other Americans had never rejected the Irish quite so much as the Irish had imagined, and perhaps the Irish, who were sensitive people, had felt rebuffs where none were intended. The problem was still real to them, and so they had to cope with it. The further problem was that the Irish were dependent on the approval of others, but often too fearful to go out and seek it. Anna McDonnell's generation — Anna herself — had been fearful, and so they had formed their own world and their own aristocracy. If the

Protestants would not accept them, then they would not accept the Protestants. It had been a wonderfully simple compromise, and it had allowed the rich Irish to live alone, follow their consciences, and through their exclusivity force the Protestants to come to them. The Murrays and McDonnells had kept the world outside the compound in Southampton, and the disdain that the Protestants had felt for the Irish interlopers turned into respect and finally envy. This was the great contribution that Anna and her generation made to the other Irish Catholics: they forced the Protestants to accept them. Once they were accepted there was no longer any need for the Irish Catholics to be as insular as they had been, but when they shed that insularity they lost something, too. When the Irish became respectable, they began acting very much like the people who had been superior to them for so long, and those special qualities that had made them Irish were put aside. They were never interred, but they were ignored, and so on the surface the Irish rich became very much like the Protestant rich. The truth, however, was that deep down the Irish were still Irish, with all the qualities that had made them Irish all along. The old Roman writers had said that the Celts were fierce, bombastic, belligerent, and sentimental, which they probably were, and qualities like that do not disappear in a generation. The chauffeurs in Southampton knew that the Murrays and McDonnells were Irish, and the chauffeurs, being Irish themselves, resented it. The Irish have always been suspicious when some of their own have gotten ahead (who do they think they are, anyway?) because they think that somehow it is a poor reflection on themselves. To get ahead, they are saying, is to be different, and to be different is to stop being Irish.

There is a nugget of truth in this, the truth being that because of being Irish they sometimes have not been allowed to get ahead. Consequently to get ahead they would simply stop being Irish. But underneath even the stuffiest of the rich Irish, and lurking within even the most frail-spirited Murray or McDonnell, there are often hints of gaiety, touches of laughter, or suggestions of stubbornness, which are some of the things that being Irish is all about. The Irish enriched our culture, and when they were not being dour, which is what being Irish can also be about, they enlivened it. Besides, no other national group ever kept its religion so faithfully as did the Irish, and even though they paid dearly for this in their psychic development, and suffered more guilt than was good for them, the Irish were monuments to fidelity. Some of the Irish rich still are monuments, although for most of them the quality of the faith is not so innocent as it once was. Years ago, Anna McDonnell took her children to Lourdes, and on coming to a pool in a grotto she told one son, an asthmatic, to stick his head in. "Mother," he said, "are you crazy?" When Anna McDonnell died in November of 1975 she left behind her thirteen children, sixty-five grandchildren, and a firm conviction among friends and relatives that they were not likely to see someone like her again. Toward the end of her life she had battled age, sickness, and everything else that flesh is heir to, and she had done it mostly by ignoring the problems and saying her prayers. Her funeral Mass was celebrated at St. Vincent Ferrer on the East Side of New York by thirteen clergymen, including a cardinal, who said that she was "a woman of good works and charity," and who couldn't say more because she had been part of an earlier age and he simply hadn't known her very well.

Anna McDonnell was the last of the Irish Catholic aristocrats in her generation, and while there may be new aristocrats tomorrow they really won't be the same. There are Irish families all over America that listen to their priests, hope their sons will get into Georgetown or Notre Dame, and are earnestly respectable in all their ways. Tomorrow they may become rich, but there will not be a society of rich Irish

Catholics for them to enter because that has disappeared. Possibly this is a good thing, but perhaps we are the poorer for it, too.

Illustrations

following page 80

Thomas E. Murray and his family in 1905 (Private collection)

The patriarch: Thomas E. Murray. Born 1860. Died 1929 (Courtesy of Mrs. Richard Harris)

Outside Thomas E. Murray's house on St. Mark's Avenue, Brooklyn, in 1906 (Courtesy of John F. Murray)

Mrs. Thomas E. Murray and three of her daughters, Catherine, Anna, and Julia, around 1915 (Courtesy of Mrs. Richard Harris)

Members of the third generation with their grandmother, Mrs. Thomas E. Murray, at her home in Brooklyn, about 1925 (Courtesy of Jeanne Murray Vanderbilt)

John F. Murray, who was called Jack, and his son John Jr. in Southampton about 1930 (Courtesy of Mrs. Sidney B. Wood, Jr.)

Anna and James McDonnell outside the Southampton Riding and Hunting Club in 1940 (Wide World Photos)

Anna and James McDonnell and their 14 children in their Fifth Avenue apartment in 1936 (Walter Scott Shinn)

The beach outside the Southampton Bathing Corporation (or, as it is usually called, the Beach Club) in 1936 (Private collection)

Coaching at the Southampton Riding and Hunting Club in the 1930s (Courtesy of Mrs. Sidney B. Wood, Jr.)

Cardinal Pacelli on his visit to America in 1936, with William Cardinal O'Connell of Boston and Francis J. Spellman (Private collection)

Henry Ford dancing with his grandson's new bride, the former Anne McDonnell, at her Southampton wedding in 1940 (Photo by Bert Morgan)

The former Jeanne Murray and Alfred Gwynne Vanderbilt just after their marriage in 1945 (Private collection)

The dining room at the Grosse Pointe Country Club on the night of Charlotte Ford's coming-out party in 1959 (*Joe Clark,* TIME-LIFE *Picture Agency © Time Inc.*)

The receiving line. Charlotte Ford, her mother, and her father, Henry Ford II (*Joe Clark,* TIME-LIFE *Picture Agency © Time Inc.*)

Charlotte Ford and Stavros Niarchos in St. Moritz after their marriage in December 1965 (Wide World Photos)

T. Murray McDonnell and his frequent guest, Jacqueline Onassis, hunting in Peapack, New Jersey, in 1968 (Wide World Photos)

Francis Cardinal Spellman and Bishop Fulton Sheen in the late 1960s (*The New York Times—Jack Manning*)

Anne McDonnell Ford and her mother, Anna McDonnell, after Mass at St. Vincent Ferrer in New York, 1967 (*The New York Times—William E. Sauro*)

The McDonnells in the late 1960s (Courtesy of Mrs. Richard Harris)

Index

Adams, Henry, 130
Adrian IV, Pope, 24
Albany, Irish in, 1–5
Albany Electric Illuminating Company, 11
Albany Gas Company, 6
Albany Gaslight Company, 10
Albany Hibernian Provident, 3
Alcohol: Irish curse of, 31; selling of, by Irish, 33–34
Allenhurst, New Jersey, 38–39
American Museum of Safety, 18
Amory, Cleveland, 84, 118, 125
Ancient Order of Hibernians, 35
Anderson, John, 1
Astor, Mrs. William Backhouse, 69–70
Atomic Energy Commission, 19, 54, 89
Austin, Christina Vettore, see Ford, Christina Vettore

Baldwin, Lucky, 63
Baltimore, Baron: third, 55; fourth, 56
Barry, Bertha, 127–29
Barry, Ida, see Ryan, Ida Barry
Barry, John S., 129
Barthelmess, Richard, 117

Baruch, Bernard, 131
Basset, Teddy, 153
Beebe, Lucius, 138
Beer, Thomas, 124–25
Bergman, Ingrid, 155
Berlin, Mr. and Mrs. Irving, 67
Bonanza, 66–67
Bonaparte, Joseph, 59
Bonding, 175
Booth, Junius Brutus, 62
Boston, Irish population of, 136–37
Bouicault, Dion, 124
Boyl, Bernard, 87
Bradley, Catherine, see Murray, Catherine Bradley
Bradley, Daniel (Honest Dan), 11–12, 14–15, 19, 37–38
Bradley, Edward Riley, 162
Brady, Anthony Nicholas, 8–10, 33, 129; electrical empire of, 10–11, 12–13; death of 44; rapid-transit operations of, 130
Brady, Diamond Jim, 137–39
Brady, Ellen Malone, 8–9
Brady, Marie, see Murray, Marie Brady
Brady, Nicholas (father of Anthony Nicholas), 8–9

Brady, Nicholas (Nick) (son of Anthony Nicholas), 44–45, 47, 91

Brady, Mrs. Nicholas, 90–92

Brandeis, Louis, 137

Brian Boru, 24

Brooklyn, Irish Catholics in, 13

Brooklyn *Eagle,* 101, 106

Broun, Heywood, 97

Brown, James J., 67, 68

Brown, "Leadville Johnny," 67

Brown, Margaret Tobin, 67–68

"Brown, unsinkable Molly," 68

Bruce, Ailsa Mellon (Mrs. David Bruce), 135

Buckley, James, 165

Budenz, Louis, 97

Bunratty Singers, 173

Burke, John, 93

Butler, James, 107

Butler, Nicholas Murray, 70–71

Butler, Patrick, 159, 163

Butler, Pierce, 159

Byers, Buckley, 53, 106, 107

Byers, Rosamund Murray (Mrs. Buckley Byers) (daughter of Joseph and Theresa Murray), 53, 106

Byrnes & McDonnell, 39

Caldwell, Mr., 58

Canterbury, 146, 168

Carey, Hugh, 164, 165

Carroll, Charles, of Annapolis, 56–57

Carroll, Charles, of Carrollton, 55, 57, 59, 135

Carroll, Charles (first, of Maryland), 55, 56

Carroll, Nina Ryan, 135

Carroll, Philip, 135

Castro, Fidel, 148

Caton, Mrs. Richard, 57–58

Cavanagh, Barbara, *see* Wagner, Barbara Cavanagh

Cavanagh, Edward, 137

Cavanagh, James, 137, 139, 163

Cavanagh, John, 137, 163

Cavanagh, Mary, 98

Cecilian Club, 167

Celestius, 23

Celts, 22–23, 185

Chappaquiddick, 172

Chicago *Post,* 31

Christy, Howard Chandler, 41, 108

Churchill family, 142

Clark, Mr. and Mrs. George Tillinghast, 65

Colby, Anita, 144–46

Cole, Nat King, 142

Coleman, John, 93

Collier, Barron, 47

Conn of the Hundred Battles, 23

Connel, John, 1

Conniff, Frank, 115

Connor family, 124–25

Consolidated Edison, 13, 15–16, 44–45, 104

Consolidated Gas Company, 13

Cooke, Terence Cardinal, 146, 164

Cooley, Richard, 120–21

Cooper, Mr. and Mrs. Gary, 142

Cormac, 23

Counihan, Daniel, 144

Courrèges, André, 152

Croker, Richard, 32

Cromwell, Oliver, 25, 27

Cuchullain, 23

Cuddihy, Julia Murray (Mrs. Lester Cuddihy) (daughter of Thomas Edward and Catherine Murray), 12, 21; engagement and marriage of, 40, 43–44; life in Water Mill home of, 71, 76,

Cuddihy, Julia Murray, *contd.* 77; death of husband of, 99–100; importance of clergy to, 99–100; illness of, 100; children of, 122–23

Cuddihy, Lester, 41, 46; engagement and marriage of, to Julia Murray, 40, 43–44; life in Water Mill home of, 71, 76; importance of clergy to, 99; death of, 99–100; children of, 122–23

Cuddihy, Mary Jane (daughter of Lester and Julia Cuddihy), 106, 107

Cuddihy, Robert (son of Lester and Julia Cuddihy), 122–23

Cuddihy, Thomas (son of Lester and Julia Cuddihy), 122–23

Cushing, Richard Cardinal, 88–89

Davenport, Charles Benedict, 125–26

Davies, Marion, 140

Davis, Meyer, 142

Debutante Cotillion, 95

Debutantes, 94–96

Delaneys and Delanos, 125

Delehanty family, 124–25

Delevan House, 4, 9

Diman, Reverend J. Hugh, 146

Dior, Christian, 152

Dirksen, Everett, 96

Dixon, Dorinda, *see* Ryan, Dorinda Dixon

Dockery, Lady, 153

Dodge, Horace, 161

Doheny, Mr. and Mrs. Edward L., 139

Dollar, Stanley, 91

Donahue, Mary Ellen, 64–65

Donahue, Mr. and Mrs. Peter, 60

Donaldson, Lufkin & Jenrette, 181

Downey, John G., 60–61

Du Barry, Madame, 68

Duke, James, 130

Dunne, Finley Peter, 70–71

Dunne, Irene, 89

Du Pont family, 142

Durand, Jeanne, *see* Murray, Jeanne Durand

Eagleton, Thomas, 181

Eden, Anthony, 116

Edison, Thomas, 6, 10, 15, 20, 47

Edison Electric Illuminating Company of New York, 10

Edison Electric Light Company, 10

Eisenhower, Dwight D., 144

Elizabeth I, 25

Elkins, William B., 130

Emerson, Margaret, 112–13

Emmet, Thomas Addis, 2–3

Emmett family, 124

Equitable Life Insurance Company, 131

Erie Canal, Irishmen working on, 3

Fair, Birdie, 66

Fair, James, 66, 69

Fair, Tessie, *see* Oelrichs, Tessie Fair

Fall, Albert, 139

Famine, Great, 27, 28–29

Faraday, Michael, 6

Farrell, James A., 39, 47

Farrell, James T., 170

Farrell, Theresa, *see* Murray, Theresa Farrell

Farrell, Thomas F., 52, 98

Finn, John, 1

Firestone family, 142

Fitzgerald, F. Scott, 112

Fitzgerald family, 166
Flagler, Palen, 145–46
Flanigan, Horace, Murray Mc-Donnell's marriage to daughter of, 120, 177
Flanigan, Peter, 180–81
Flood, James, 66
Flynn, Ed, 110
Ford, Anne (later Mrs. Giancarlo Uzielli) (daughter of Henry and Anne Ford), 146, 150–51, 183; education and early life of, 142–43, 147–50; residence of, on Park Avenue, 152; marriage of, 156
Ford, Anne McDonnell, *see* Johnson, Anne McDonnell
Ford, Charlotte (daughter of Henry and Anne Ford), 146, 183, 184; coming-out party for, 141–42; education and early life of, 142–43, 147–50; and Stavros Niarchos, 150–57 *passim;* residence of, on Park Avenue, 152; pregnancy of, 153–54, 155–56; marriage to and separation from Niarchos, 157
Ford, Christina Vettore (Mrs. Henry Ford), marriage of, 119–20, 153
Ford, Edsel, 101, 103, 104, 105
Ford, Mrs. Edsel, 101, 104, 117
Ford, Henry (grandfather of Henry Ford II), 103, 104, 105
Ford, Henry, II, 20, 28, 52, 86, 97; marriage of, to Anne McDonnell, 101–6, 141; and Buckley Byers, 107; breakup of his marriage to Anne, 117–20, 152; marriage of, to Christina Austin, 119–20, 153; and daughter Charlotte's coming-out party, 142; and Stavros Niarchos,

Ford, Henry, II, *contd.*
153–54, 156–57; and McDonnell & Company, 180
Ford, John, 28
Ford Motor Company, 153, 180
Forrest, Edwin, 63
Freud, Sigmund, 38

Georgetown Law School, 38
Georgetown University, 18, 154–55
Gibbons, James Cardinal, 87–88
Gold and silver camps, Irish fortunes made in, 65–66
Gotham Ball, 95–96
Gould, Jay, 43
Grace, Peter, 91, 96
Grace, Princess, of Monaco, 158, 163, 164, 165, 173–74
Grant, Ulysses S., 67
Greeley, Father Andrew M., 169, 170
Gregory, Mr. and Mrs. John H., 65
Guinness, Peter, 135

Haggerty, Harry, 93
Haggerty, Laura, 121
Harper's Bazaar, 118
Harrigan, Edward, 34
Harris, Basil, 91, 92, 107–8
Harris, Basil, Jr., 92; marriage of, to Marie Murray, 107
Harris, Charlotte McDonnell (Mrs. Richard Harris) (daughter of James and Anna McDonnell), 73, 108, 143
Harris, Marie Murray (Mrs. Basil Harris, Jr.) (daughter of Thomas E. and Marie Murray, Jr.), 46, 72–73; coming-out party for, 85–86; marriage of, 106–7

Hart, Tony, 34
Hartington, Marquess of, 168
Hayes, Patrick Cardinal, 93, 107
Hearst, William Randolph, 84
Henry II, 24
Henry VIII, 25
Henry, Joseph, 6
Herbert, Victor, 39
Hibernia Bank, 60
History, Irish, 22–29
Hogan, William, 1
Holm, Eleanor, 86
Hone, Philip, 59
Hughes, Bishop John, 29
Hurley, Brother, 99

Insull, Samuel, 47
Ireland, Archbishop John, 87–88
Irish American Cultural Institute, 159, 163, 164, 165, 173
Irish Freedom Movement, 139
Irish *Times,* 159–60
Irish Tourist Board, 173
Irving, Kitty, 73
Irving, Washington, 73

James II, 25, 55–56
Javits, Marian and Jacob, 164
Jenny Lind Theaters, 62
Jerome, St., 23
Johnson, Anne McDonnell (Mrs. Dean Johnson) (daughter of James and Anna McDonnell) (former wife of Henry Ford II), 52, 86, 153, 184; marriage of, to Henry Ford, 101–6, 141; breakup of her marriage, 117–20; and daughter Charlotte's coming-out party, 142; residence of, on Park Avenue, 152; and daughter Charlotte's pregnancy, 155–56; marriage of, to Dean Johnson, 181

Johnson, Dean, 181
Johnson, Dr. Samuel, 30
Jones, Alice, 128
Jung, Carl, 49
Junior Assemblies, 95, 96
Junior League, 167

Kahn, Margaret, *see* Ryan, Margaret Kahn
Kahn, Otto H., 135, 147
Keenan, Paddy, 6
Keene, James R., 131
Keller, Father, 96, 102, 111, 123
Keller, Louie, 127
Kelly, Grace, *see* Grace, Princess, of Monaco
Kelly, John, 165
Kennedy, Edward, 164, 168, 171, 172
Kennedy, Eunice, 104
Kennedy, Joan, 172
Kennedy, John F., 104, 108, 118, 165, 168, 170–71
Kennedy, Joseph P., 108, 136, 166, 167, 169; appointed Ambassador to England, 74; contributions of, to Archdiocese of Boston, 89; education of his children, 168
Kennedy, Joseph P., Jr., 104, 168, 170
Kennedy, Kathleen, 104, 168
Kennedy, Robert F., 108, 168
Kennedy, Rose, 104, 166–72; her friendship with Anna McDonnell, 73–74, 78, 166; time spent in Ireland by, 165–66
Kennedy family, 164, 170
Kenny, William F., 47
Killeen, Father George, 86, 99, 102, 154; his friendship with Murrays and McDonnells, 80–82, 90; Henry Ford on, 117;

Killeen, Father George, *contd.*
refusal of, to bury children of divorced parents, 121
King, Captain Richard, 139

Lace-curtain Irish, 34
Ladies' Home Journal, 118
Lafayette, Marquis de, 4
Langtree, Tom, 43, 51
Laoghaire, 23
Lawford, Mrs. Peter, 118
Lee, Robert E., 139
Legends, 23
Lehman, Herbert H., 83
Leo XIII, Pope, 88
Leopold, King, of Belgium, 130–31
Lewis, Frank J., Milk Fund, 95
Life magazine, 141, 143
Lind, Jenny, 5
Literary Digest, 40
Livanos, George, 151
Livanos, Tina, *see* Onassis, Tina Livanos
Livingston, Mrs. Goodhue, 70
London *Times,* 29
Longworth Medal, of Franklin Institute, 18
Louis, Sherry, 86, 95
Luce, Clare Booth, 97, 98
Lufkin, Dan, 181–82
Lufkin, Elgood, 182
Lufkin, Marie Murray (Mrs. Elgood Lufkin) (daughter of Thomas Edward and Catherine Murray), 14, 21, 71, 123; first marriage of, to John McDonnell, 42; second marriage of, to Elgood Lufkin, 182
Lynch, Dominick (father), 58
Lynch, Dominick (son), 58–59

McAllister, Ward, 58
McCloskey, John Cardinal, 4, 13
McCormack, John, 6
McDonald, John B., 33
McDonnell, Anna Murray (Mrs. James McDonnell) (daughter of Thomas Edward and Catherine Murray), 12, 20–21, 38, 43, 45–46; and Bishop Sheen, 14, 52, 98; marriage of, 39, 42, 175; family life of, 50–51; life in Southampton home of, 71, 76, 77–78, 79, 143; her friendship with Rose Kennedy, 73–74, 166; elegance of, 78; faith of, 79–80, 183, 184; and Father Killeen, 80; and Cardinal Pacelli, 92; and Cardinal Spellman, 92; and Gotham Ball, 95; and daughter Anne's marriage to Henry Ford, 101–6; resentment of, toward Jack Murray's family, 109; and Jeanne Murray's marriage to Alfred Gwynne Vanderbilt, 111; divorces among children of, 121; residence of, on Park Avenue, 152; and collapse of McDonnell & Company, 181, 183, 184; contribution of, to Irish Catholics, 185; death of, 186
McDonnell, Anne, *see* Johnson, Anne McDonnell
McDonnell, Catherine, *see* Sullivan, Catherine McDonnell
McDonnell, Charles (son of James and Anna McDonnell), 177
McDonnell, Gerald (son of James and Anna McDonnell), 121
McDonnell, James (husband of Anna Murray McDonnell), 42, 43, 45; marriage of, 39; uprightness of, 46; family life of,

McDonnell, James, *contd.*
50–51; life in Southampton home of, 71, 76, 77; and Father Killeen, 80; and Cardinal Pacelli, 92; and daughter Anne's marriage to Henry Ford, 102–6; and Jeanne Murray's marriage to Alfred Gwynne Vanderbilt, 111; divorces among children of, 121; and McDonnell & Company, 175–77; death of, 176, 177

McDonnell, Jim (son of James and Anna McDonnell), 43, 51, 105

McDonnell, John, marriage of, to Marie Murray, 42

McDonnell, Marie Murray, *see* Lufkin, Marie Murray

McDonnell, Marjorie (daughter of James and Anna McDonnell), 108

McDonnell, Murray (son of James and Anna McDonnell), 119; marriage of, to daughter of Horace Flanigan, 120, 177; and collapse of McDonnell & Company, 177–78, 180–82, 184

McDonnell, Peter (father of James McDonnell), 175

McDonnell, Sean (son of James and Anna McDonnell), 106, 179–80

McDonnell, Sheila (daughter of James and Anna McDonnell), 120–21

McDonnell & Company, 39, 119, 120, 175–78; collapse of, 178–82, 183, 184

McDonnells, general references to, 45, 55, 72, 73, 75, 141, 163, 185, 186

McGee, Thomas D'Arcy, 31

MacGuire, James, 106, 107

Mackay, Clarence Hungerford, 38, 67

Mackay, Ellin, 67

Mackay, John, 33, 38, 66–67

Mackay, Mrs. John, 67

McKenna, Irene, 133

McKiernan, Eoin, 159

McLaughlin, Patrick, 65

McLean, Edward Beale, 140

McLean, Evalyn Walsh, 140

McMullen, Nora, *see* Mellon, Nora McMullen

MacMurrough, Dermot, 24

MacNessa, Conor, 23

McQuail, Catherine Murray (Mrs. John Ennis McQuail) (daughter of Thomas Edward and Catherine Murray), 12, 20, 21, 45–46, 77; marriage of, 40; move to Southampton by, 71; separation from her husband, 71, 81; and Father Killeen, 81

McQuail, John Ennis, 46; marriage of, to Catherine Murray, 40; separation of, from Catherine, 71, 81

McSorley, Father, 100

Maguire, Little Em, 62, 63

Maguire, Tom, 62–64

Maguire's Opera House, 62–64

Mann, "Colonel" William D'Alton, 131

Martin, Mr. and Mrs. Edward, 60

Maxwell, George, 133

Meiggs, Henry, 61–62

Mellon, Ailsa, *see* Bruce, Ailsa Mellon

Mellon, Andrew, 135–36

Mellon, Nora McMullen, 135–36

Mellon, Paul, 135

Metropolitan Device Company, 44–45

Metropolitan Street Railway Company, 131

Migration, of Irish to America, 27–29

Molloy, Archbishop Thomas E., 47, 53, 79

Money, Irish attitude toward, 32–33

Montesquieu, on Penal Laws, 26

Montezemolo, Cathie Murray di (Mrs. Alesandro Montezemolo) (daughter of John and Jeanne Murray), 72, 144

Moran, Mr. and Mrs. Daniel, 161–62

Morgan, J. Pierpont, 13, 131, 137

Morgan, Nan, *see* Ryan, Nan Morgan

Morris, Robert, 107

Morrisey, John, 32

Municipal Gaslight Company, 11

Murphy, Don Timoteo, 60

Murphy, Patrick Francis, 70–71

Murphys and Murfies, 125

Murray, Anastasia (mother of Thomas Edward Murray), 6–7

Murray, Anna, *see* McDonnell, Anna Murray

Murray, Bradley (son of Thomas E. and Marie Murray, Jr.), 123

Murray, Catherine, *see* McQuail, Catherine Murray

Murray, Catherine Bradley (Mrs. Thomas Edward Murray), 7, 21, 45–46; her marriage to Thomas Murray, 11–12; birth of children of, 12; disciplining of children by, 14; death of, 46

Murray, Cathie, *see* Montezemolo, Cathie Murray di

Murray, Constance (daughter of John and Jeanne Murray), 123

Murray, Daniel (son of Thomas Edward and Catherine Murray), 12, 20, 40, 41; life of, spent in mental institutions, 19, 38, 48

Murray, Jeanne, *see* Vanderbilt, Jeanne Murray

Murray, Jeanne Durand (Mrs. John Murray), 45–46; marriage of, 40–41, 108; death of husband of, 82–84; marriage of daughters of, 107, 108, 109; divorces among children of, 121–22; death of, 123

Murray, Jimmy (son of Thomas E. and Marie Murray, Jr.), 46

Murray, John (brother of Thomas Edward Murray), 6

Murray, John (father of Thomas Edward Murray), 5–6

Murray, John (son of John and Jeanne Murray), 121–22

Murray, John (Jack) (son of Thomas Edward and Catherine Murray), 12, 19–20, 45–46, 99, 123; marriage of, to Jeanne Durand, 40–41, 108; moodiness of, 41–42; his interest in politics, 48–49; Wall Street venture of, 49; drinking problem of, 49–50; life in Southampton home of, 71, 76; and Father Killeen, 82; illness and death of, 82–84; marriage of daughters of, 107, 108, 109; divorces among children of, 121–22

Murray, John Courtney (theologian), 90

Murray, Joseph B. (son of Thomas Edward and Catherine Murray), 12, 19, 42–43, 44–45; marriage of, to Theresa Farrell, 39; compared with his

Murray, Joseph B., *contd.*
brothers, 46; marriage of daughter of, 53–54, 106; Southampton home of, 71; children of, 77, 121

Murray, Julia, *see* Cuddihy, Julia Murray

Murray, Marie (daughter of Thomas Edward and Catherine Murray), *see* Lufkin, Marie Murray

Murray, Marie (daughter of Thomas E. and Marie Murray Jr.), *see* Harris, Marie Murray

Murray, Marie Brady (Mrs. Thomas E. Murray, Jr.), 42, 53, 78; marriage of, 39–40; Southampton home of, 71; and private chapel of Thomas E. Murray, Jr., 79–80; and Father Killeen, 80; coming-out party for daughter of, 85–86; and Gotham Ball, 95

Murray, Patricia, *see* Wood, Patricia Murray

Murray, Rosamund, *see* Byers, Rosamund Murray

Murray, Theresa Farrell (Mrs. Joseph B. Murray), 42, 45; marriage of, 39; marriage of daughter of, 53–54, 106; Southampton home of, 71; children of, 77, 121

Murray, Thomas Edward, 22, 37, 52, 84, 164, 168; birth of, 5; early life of, 5–8; influence of mother on, 6–7; his genius with machines, 8, 16–18; and Anthony Nicholas Brady, 8, 10, 11, 130; first jobs of, 10, 11; his marriage to Catherine Bradley, 11–12; birth of children of, 12; and Brady's electrical em-

Murray, Thomas Edward, *contd.*
pire, 12–13; his move to Brooklyn, 13–14; design of power plants by, 15; inventions of, 15–18; piety of, 18, 184; attitude toward Protestants of, 18–19; children of, 19–21, 36, 38–54; impact of Prohibition on, 44; and Metropolitan Device Company, 44–45; Sunday dinners at home of, 45; death of wife of, 46; death and funeral of, 46–48, 76, 169; Southampton home of, 71; fireworks display put on by, 74–75; number of grandchildren of, 122; great-grandchildren of, 141, 143; importance of work and the church to, 182–83

Murray, Thomas E., Jr. (son of Thomas Edward and Catherine Murray), 12, 42, 44–45; and Atomic Energy Commission, 19, 54, 89; marriage of, to Marie Brady, 39–40; compared with his brothers, 46; fire in home of, 46; and Interborough Rapid Transit Company, 48–49; piety of, 52–53; his reaction to niece's marriage to Protestant, 54, 106; life in Southampton home of, 71, 74, 76, 77, 143; private chapel of, 79–80; and Father Killeen, 80, 82; coming-out party for daughter of, 85–86; his consultations with John Courtney Murray, 89–90; affiliation with Jesuits of, 98–99; marriage of daughter of, 106–7; resentment of, toward Jack Murray's family, 109; and Jeanne Murray's mar-

Murray, Thomas E., Jr., *contd.*
riage to Alfred Gwynne Vanderbilt, 110; children of, 123
Murray, Tommy (son of Thomas
E. and Marie Murray, Jr.), 46,
52
Murray Conduit Systems, 48
Murray Manufacturing Company,
41
Murray Radiator Company, 48
Murrays, general references to,
55, 72, 73, 75, 141, 163, 185,
186

Nast, Thomas, 29–30
National Cigarette Company, 130
Nevils, Monsignor Coleman, 53–
54
New York, Irish population of,
30–31
New York *Daily News,* 104, 116,
164, 173
New York *Evening Post,* 59
New York *Herald Tribune,* 84
New York Foundling Hospital, 95
New York Stock Exchange, 178,
179
New York Times, 7, 84, 96, 149,
169
Newman, John Cardinal, 166
Newport, Rhode Island, 69–70
Niall of the Nine Hostages, 23
Niarchos, Eugenia, 155, 156, 157
Niarchos, Stavros, 20; and Char-
lotte Ford, 150–57; and Henry
Ford, 153–54. *See also* Ford,
Charlotte
Nicoll, Mary T., 132
Nixon, Richard M., 180
Noonan, Reverend D. P., 96–97
Nutting, Anthony, 115–16

O'Brien, Lawrence, 180, 181
O'Brien, Judge Morgan, 70–71
O'Brien, William, 66
O'Briens and Bryants, 125
O'Byrne, Mother, 172
Occasional Thinkers, 70–71
O'Connell, William Cardinal, 88,
89, 90, 92, 125, 170
O'Donnell family, 124–25
Oelrichs, Hermann, 66
Oelrichs, Tessie Fair, 66, 69–70,
79
O'Farrell, Jasper, 60
Ogilvy, Lord David, 135
Ogilvy, Virginia Ryan, 135
O'Hara, John, 170
O'Mahaney, Monsignor, 162
Onassis, Aristotle, 151
Onassis, Jacqueline, 120, 151,
177, 178
Onassis, Tina Livanos, 151
O'Neill, Eugene, 64, 170
O'Neill, Hugh (Earl of Tyrone),
25
O'Neill, James, 64
O'Reilly, John Boyle, 108
O'Riley, Peter, 65

Pacelli, Eugenio Cardinal (later
Pope Pius XII), 91–92, 97, 107
Paley, William S. and Babe, 112,
115
Parvel, Thomas, 1
Passavant Cotillion, 95
Patrick, St., 23
Patton, Elizabeth, 125–26
Paul, Maury, 84
Paulist Fathers, notice for Irish
parishioners from, 35–36
Payne, Flora, *see* Whitney, Flora
Payne
Payton, Father, 96
Penal Laws, 25–27, 32, 113

Peoples Gaslight Company, 10
Phelan, James (father), 61
Phelan, James (son), 61
Pierre, Hotel, dinner for Irish Americans at, 158–59, 163, 164, 173–74
Pilot, The, 108
Pius V, Pope, 25
Pius X, Pope, 132
Pius XI, Pope, 97
Pius XII, Pope, 92, 97–98, 105, 143, 166
Platt, Harry, 153
Players Club, 43, 99
Portsmouth Priory, 146, 150, 168
Post, Emily, 128
Preston, John, 125–26
Prohibition, 44

Quigg, Mr., 131

Rhinelander, Leonard Kip, 128
Rickenbacker, Eddie, 145
Rights, brokerage houses specializing in, 176
Roche, Arthur Somers, 108
Roche, Deirdre, 121
Roche, James Jeffrey, 108
Roche, Jeffrey; marriage of, to Patricia Murray, 107, 108; divorce of, from Patricia, 121
Roche, Patricia Murray, *see* Wood, Patricia Murray
Rockefeller, William, 13
Rodin, François Auguste René, 131
Roosevelt, Franklin Delano, 48, 92
Roosevelt family, 142
Rose, Billy, 86
Rossellini, Roberto, 155
Russell, Lillian, 138

Russell, Rosalind, 89, 145
Ryan, Allan, 132–33
Ryan, Clendenin, 132, 134
Ryan, Clendenin, Jr., 134
Ryan, Dorinda Dixon, 135
Ryan, Ida Barry, 129, 131–32
Ryan, John Barry, 132, 133–34, 135
Ryan, John Barry, Jr., 135
Ryan, John Barry, III, 135
Ryan, Joseph, 132
Ryan, Margaret Kahn, 135
Ryan, Nan Morgan, 133
Ryan, Nina, *see* Carroll, Nina Ryan
Ryan, Thomas Fortune, 38, 70, 129, 130–32, 139, 163; sons of, 132–34; grandchildren of, 134–35
Ryan, Virginia, *see* Ogilvy, Virginia Ryan
Ryan, William Kane, 132

Sacred Heart, Order of the, 146–50
Sage, Russell, 13
St. Andrew's Society, 2
St. Edward's Church (Palm Beach), 162
St. Mary's Church (Albany), 4
St. Patrick's Day celebrations, 2–3, 30, 161–63
St. Patrick's Society, 2
San Francisco, Irish population of, 59–65, 66
San Francisco *Morning Call*, 65
Schiff, Gloria O'Connor, 144
Schroeder, Baron Henry von, 64–65
Self-destruction, Irish, 170
Selznick, David O., 144
Shannon, William, 136
Shaw, George Bernard, 160

Sheen, Bishop Fulton J., 14, 52, 96–98; and marriage of Anne McDonnell and Henry Ford, 102, 104–5, 106

Simpson, Wallis, 101

Smith, Al, 47, 77, 83, 92, 106

Social Register, 124, 127–29

Society for the Propagation of the Faith, 52, 97

Southampton Club, 70–71

Spalding, Archbishop Martin, 4, 87–88

Spellman, Francis Cardinal, 88, 91–94, 143, 164; and Gotham Ball, 95–96; and Fulton J. Sheen, 97–98; and Anita Colby, 145; scroll presented to Rose Kennedy by, 166

Statute of Kilkenny, 24

Strong, George Templeton, 31

Stutz Motor Car Company, 132–33

Sullivan, Catherine McDonnell (Mrs. R. Peter Sullivan) (daughter of James and Anna McDonnell), 103, 111; marriage of, to R. Peter Sullivan, 106, 107

Sullivan, John L., 32

Sullivan, R. Peter, marriage of, to Catherine McDonnell, 106, 107

Synge, John Millington, 35

Talcott, General Sebastian Vissher, 7–8, 45

Talleyrand, 4

Teapot Dome scandal, 139

Tennyson, Alfred Lord, 29

Tilton, Newell, 77, 117–18

Time magazine, 144

Titanic, 68

Town Topics, 131

Twain, Mark, 125

Twombly, Florence, 51

Union Club, 71

Union Tobacco Company, 130

United Irish and Scotch Benevolent Society, 2

United Shoe Machinery Corporation, 137

Uzielli, Anne Ford, *see* Ford, Anne

Uzielli, Giancarlo, marriage of, to Anne Ford, 156

Vanderbilt, Alfred, Sr., 112

Vanderbilt, Alfred Gwynne, 20, 72; marriage of, to Jeanne Murray, 109–14, 128–29; breakup of his marriage, 114–15, 116–17

Vanderbilt, Alfred Gwynne, Jr., 113–14

Vanderbilt, Heidi, 113

Vanderbilt, Jeanne Murray (Mrs. Alfred Gwynne Vanderbilt) (daughter of John and Jeanne Murray), 72; marriage of, to Alfred Gwynne Vanderbilt, 109–14, 128–29; breakup of her marriage, 114–17; and Anthony Nutting, 115–16

Vanderbilt, Mr. and Mrs. William K., 66

Van Rensselaer family, 7

Vogue, 72, 142

Von Moltke, Helmuth, 65

Wagner, Barbara Cavanagh, 137

Wagner, Robert, 137

Wales, Prince of, 67

Walker, James, 66
Walker, James J., 47, 93
Wall Street Journal, 179
Walsh Evayln, *see* McLean, Evalyn Walsh
Walsh, Tom, 139–40
Washington, George, 57, 58
Washington *Post,* 140
WASPs, 158–59, 161, 166
Wecter, Dixon, 128
Weidenfeld, George, 164
Whitney, Betsey, 112
Whitney, Flora Payne, 129, 133
Whitney, John Hay, 112, 128–29
Whitney, William Collins, 129–31
Widener, Peter A. B., 129, 130
Wiederman, Miss, 46
Wilde, Oscar, 63

William of Orange, 56
Windsor, Duke of, 101
Women's Wear Daily, 173
Wood, Patricia Murray (Mrs. Sidney Wood) (daughter of John and Jeanne Murray); marriage of, to Jeffrey Roche, 107, 108; divorce of, from Roche, 121; marriage of, to Sidney Wood, 121
Wood, Sidney B., 121
Wood, Sidney, III, 121

Yeats, William Butler, 35
Yerkes, Charles T., 131
Young, Loretta, 145

Ziegler, Ron, 181